We who live now face a constellation of intertangled crises, each of which demands the multidisciplinary collaboration so powerfully exemplified by the contributors here, in works of imagination and scholarship . . . *Cloud Climbers* is a collection of pithy, passionate and heartfelt calls, in visual art, poetry, and prose, to urgent and effective action. Essential reading for the common good now, and a just, peaceful and sustainable future.

Duncan Reid
Author of *Time We Started Listening: Theological Questions Put to Us by Recent Indigenous Writing.*

———————

Cloud Climbers mobilises the transformational potential of the Arts to generate social change, doing the needed heart-work of honouring and grieving for what and those who have suffered, as well as imagining vibrant possibilities of just and sustainable peace for all.

Anne M Carson
Poet and visual artist, author of *Massaging Himmler: A Poetic Biography of Dr Felix Kersten.*

———————

Shifting into emphatic communitarian responsiveness, the exemplary thinkers in this anthology show us not only how to hope, indeed how to 'become capable' of acting. These 'cloud climbers' create a powerful gestalt which is as creatively savvy as it is critically truthful, their engaged ethics sharply intelligent in ways that remain painstakingly, generously human.

Dan Disney
Poet and professor, Sogang University, Seoul; co-editor of *Writing to the Wire.*

Praise for **William Kelly**'s art

Kelly, in a quiet, but consistent manner has devoted his life and art to the peace movement and is widely considered as the moral conscience of Australian art. He is a gifted, and at times brilliant, natural draughtsman, who frequently weaves his compositions together like a tapestry allowing the accumulated power of images to develop a singular, strong and dominant voice. ... In a world that sometimes appears to be hurtling along a path of self-destruction ... Bill Kelly's art [is] a strong affirmation that art has the power to alter society and to join the ranks of those who are fighting the good fight. It is critical for us to remember that despite all obstacles, peace must win, as the alternative is too frightening to even contemplate.

Sasha Grishin

Professor Emeritus, Australian National University
Excerpts, 'Give Peace a Chance', Grishin's Art Blog, December 2016

———————

A deep and respectful understanding of the human experience defines William Kelly and is at the core of his art practice and his remarkable artwork. For almost five decades he has created work that engages audiences to reflect on issues of violence, war and trauma and to be open to the endless possibilities of resolution through peaceful and collaborative means. Kelly does not stand in the corner with a loudspeaker shouting and directing his world view. He is more intelligent and poetic than that. He is an artist and a humanist who understands that sitting down and talking and explaining our differences and celebrating our commonalities is more productive, more rewarding and more effective. His art has always been serious, honest and confronting. However, it is not loud and controversial. Instead, it is gentle, quiet and contemplative. It asks us to stop, look, think, consider and act not via direction but rather by dialogue.

Vincent Alessi

Senior Lecturer, Creative Arts, La Trobe University, excerpts from
'Peace or War/The Big Picture, A Personal Insight', catalogue foreword,
William Kelly installation, State Library of Victoria, September 2016

———

ISBN 978-0-6488551-3-2
First Palaver edition
published June 2021
Typeface: Tiempos (Klim)
Design: Ian Robertson
Printing: IngramSpark

For additional information,
bulk or educational purchases,
and other resources, please contact
Ethica Projects, Pty. Ltd
c/o Paul Komesaroff
paul.komesaroff@monash.edu

palaver

www.palaver.com
Palaver is an imprint of
Ethica Projects, Pty Ltd.
10 Barnato Grove Armadale
Victoria 3143 Australia

Cloud Climbers

Declarations through Images and Words
for a Just and Ecologically Sustainable Peace

With artwork by
William Kelly & **Benjamin McKeown**

Edited by **Anne Elvey**

Earth at Peace Project Melbourne Australia

Joseph Camilleri
Jim Crosthwaite
Wanda Deifelt
Marie Dennis
Garry Worete Deverell
Anne Elvey
Susan Fealy
Deborah Guess
Deborah Hart
Jione Havea
Andy Jackson
Jason Kelly
William Kelly
Jonathan Keren-Black
Bella Li
Rose Lucas
Mónica A. Maher
Freya Mathews
Benjamin McKeown
Ruth Mitchell
Mick Pope
Dianne Rayson
Omar Sakr
Anna Sakurai
Craig Santos Perez
Alex Skovron
Deborah Storie
Kanchana Weerakoon
Asmi Wood

PALAVER 2021

Contents

William Kelly

Tender Dreams / Tentative Futures II
2010, digital print on archival paper, 29.5 x 21 cm.
(edition of 30)

Dreams on a Flag
1983, silkscreen on offset lithograph flag image,
c. 56 x 38 cm. (edition of 2)

Childhoods
2018, lithograph, 19 x 15 cm. (edition of 20)
Printed at the Australian Print Workshop.

The Arrival
2014, hybrid print: linocut, digital relief print
on archival paper, 12 x 18 cm.
(edition of 3)

Peace Not War / Bridge Builders
c. 2018, digital print on archival paper, 37.5 x 28.5 cm.
(edition of 10)

Dialogue II: Religion
1987–1993, silkscreen, 61 x 80 cm. (edition of 50)

Witness / Cloud Climbers II
2018, hybrid print: lithograph / digital print,
hand coloured on archival paper, 29.5 x 21 cm.
(edition of 8)

Benjamin McKeown & William Kelly

Journeys and Destinations
1999, linocut, 42.5 x 60 cm.
Produced for the United Nations
50th Anniversary of the Universal Declaration
of Human Rights Folio.

Closing the Gap
2018, hybrid linocut/digital print
on archival paper, 29.5 x 42 cm.
(edition of 15)

All works are copyright and courtesy of the artists.

Joseph Camilleri is Emeritus Professor at La Trobe University, where he held the Chair in International Relations (1994–2012), and was founding Director of the Centre for Dialogue 2006–2012. He is a Fellow of the Australian Academy of Social Sciences. He has authored or edited some thirty major books and written over 100 book chapters and journal articles covering dialogue and conflict resolution, security, the role of religion and culture in society, multiculturalism in Australia, and the politics of the Asia-Pacific region.

Jim Crosthwaite co-founded Journeys for Climate Justice with Kanchana Weerakoon. He worked as an environmental economist for many years, and now uses these skills in support of campaigns for a just transition to a fossil-free future. His writing on climate, biodiversity, economics and more can be found online at https://crosthwaite.squarespace.com/. Jim also teaches postural awareness and stress relief based on the Alexander Technique.

Wanda Deifelt is a Brazilian theologian and scholar currently teaching at Luther College in Decorah, Iowa, USA. Her areas of expertise are contextual theologies (primarily liberation, feminist and interreligious), embodiment and interdisciplinary studies.

Marie Dennis serves on the executive committee of Pax Christi's Catholic Nonviolence Initiative. She was co-president of Pax Christi International from 2007 to 2019 and is now a senior advisor to the secretary general. Marie was director for 15 years of the Maryknoll Office for Global Concerns. She is author or co-author of seven books, editor of the award-winning Orbis Book, *Choosing Peace: The Catholic Church Returns to Gospel Nonviolence,* and co-editor of *Advancing Nonviolence and Just Peace in the Church and the World* published by Pax Christi International in 2020.

Garry Worete Deverell is a trawloolway man from northern Tasmania and Vice-Chancellor's Fellow in Indigenous Theologies at Melbourne's University of Divinity. He is the author of *Gondwana Theology* (Morning Star 2018) and *The Bonds of Freedom* (Paternoster 2008).

Anne Elvey lives on Boonwurrung Country in Seaford, Victoria. Her poetry publications include, *On arrivals of breath* (Poetica Christi 2019), *White on White* (Cordite Books 2018), and *Kin* (FIP 2014), shortlisted in the New South Wales Premier's Literary Awards 2015. *Obligations of Voice* is forthcoming from Recent Work Press in 2021. Anne is editor of *hope for whole: poets speak up to Adani.* Her most recent scholarly book is *Reading the Magnificat in Australia: Unsettling Engagements* (Sheffield Phoenix 2020). Anne is an adjunct research fellow in the School of Languages, Literatures, Cultures and Linguistics, Monash University, and an honorary research associate, Trinity College Theological School, and member of the Network for Religion and Social Policy, University of Divinity.

Susan Fealy is a Melbourne-based poet and clinical psychologist. Her poems have been published in Australian journals and anthologies including *Best Australian Poems 2009, 2010, 2013* and *2017.* Others appear in the United States, India and Sweden. Among awards for her poetry are the NSW Society of Women Writers National Poetry Prize and the Henry Kendall Poetry Award. Her first collection, *Flute of Milk* (UWAP), won the 2017 Wesley Michel Wright Prize and shortlisted for the 2018 Mary Gilmore Prize. A bi-lingual volume of her poetry, *The Earthing of Rain* (Flying Island Books 2019), was translated into Chinese by Iris Fan Xing.

Deborah Guess is a Research Associate at Pilgrim Theological College, University of Divinity and Member of the Network for Religion and Social Policy, University of Divinity. Her main research and teaching focus is ecological theology. She has co-edited three volumes in relation to ecology and peace, the most recent being: Joseph Camilleri and Deborah Guess (eds), *Towards a Just and Ecologically Sustainable Peace: Navigating the Great Transition* (Singapore: Palgrave Macmillan 2020).

Deborah Hart is an arts-focused activist writer from Melbourne. After 16 years working in development roles with leading Australian arts and culture organisations, Deborah left her profession to found LIVE (Locals Into Victoria's Environment, 2006) and later co-founded CLIMARTE (2010) and ClimActs (2013) to harness the creative arts and combine spectacle, humour and direct action to draw attention to the climate emergency. Deborah is the author of *Guarding Eden* (Allen & Unwin 2015) which tells inspiring personal stories showing how ordinary citizens are powerfully collaborating across many communities to safeguard nature and humanity's future.

Jione Havea is a native pastor (Methodist Church in Tonga) and co-parent for a 7-year-old who is troubled by Disney's *Moana* (2016). We are migrants that live, work, play and dream around the land of the Wurundjeri nation. We live for and because of stories, written and oral. We tell and twist stories, and stories twist and pinch us back. Before COVID, we participated regularly in the gatherings of the Society of Biblical Literature, Oceania Biblical Studies Association, Society of Asian Biblical Studies, DARE (Discernment and Radical Engagement) and Talanoa Oceania.

Andy Jackson has featured at literary events and arts festivals in Australia, Ireland, India, and the USA. His first book of poems, *Among the Regulars*, was shortlisted for the 2011 Kenneth Slessor Prize for Poetry, and his recent collection, *Music Our Bodies Can't Hold*, portrait poems of people with Marfan Syndrome, was shortlisted for the 2020 John Bray Poetry Award. Andy's 2019 creative PhD thesis, *Disabling Poetics: Bodily Otherness and the Saying of Poetry*, was awarded a Doctoral Research Medal for Outstanding Academic Achievement by the University of Adelaide. He has co-edited disability-themed issues of the literary journals *Southerly* and *Australian Poetry Journal*, and works as a creative writing teacher and mentor for community organisations and universities.

Jason Kelly is a Mutti Mutti, Wamba Wamba man, community elected member for the First Peoples' Assembly for the North West of Victoria.

William Kelly is an artist, pacifist, husband and father. Having once called a park bench home, he is a former steel worker, truck driver, Fulbright Scholar and former Dean at the Victorian College of the Arts, Melbourne. He is now recognised internationally as a leading artist/activist whose aspirations for a more compassionate and environmentally sustainable world resonate throughout his artistic enterprise and life — leading to his receiving awards for human rights and social justice on three continents. His work is the subject of a feature film *Can Art Stop a Bullet? William Kelly's Big Picture*. Having grown up in New York, he now lives in and maintains a studio on Yorta Yorta Country in a small 'bush town' in rural Australia.

Jonathan Keren-Black is Rabbi at the Leo Baeck Centre for Progressive Judaism in East Kew, Victoria, a founder member of JECO (the Jewish Ecological Coalition) and GreenFaith Australia, and has been a member of ARRCC's (Australian Religion Response to Climate Change) management committee. https://lbc.org.au/rabbi-jonathan/

Bella Li is a writer and editor with a PhD in creative writing and literary studies. Her first book, *Argosy* (Vagabond Press 2017), won both the 2018 Victorian and NSW Premier's Literary Awards for Poetry. Her second book, *Lost Lake* (Vagabond Press 2018), was shortlisted for the 2018 QLD Literary Award for Poetry. Her writing and artwork have been published widely, including in *Best Australian Poems*, *The Kenyon Review* and *Archives of American Art Journal*.

Rose Lucas is a Melbourne poet and academic at Victoria University who lives and works on unceded Wurundjeri land. Her first collection, *Even in the Dark* (UWAP 2013), won the Mary Gilmore Award, and was followed by *Unexpected Clearing* (UWAP 2016). *This Shuttered Eye*, a study of poetry and the visual, was published by Girls on Key Press in 2021. She is currently working on a collaborative project with visual artist Sharon Monagle, '2020 Shelter in Place', and a new poetry collection *Increments of the Everyday*.

Mónica A. Maher lives in Quito, Ecuador where she teaches in the Gender, Violence and Human Rights Program of the Latin American Faculty of Social Sciences (FLACSO) and coordinates the Latin American Program of Friends Peace Teams. A Zen Sensei and Minister in the United Church of Christ, she holds a PhD from Union Theological Seminary and MDiv from Harvard Divinity School.

Freya Mathews is Emeritus Professor of Environmental Philosophy at Latrobe University and a fellow of the Australian Academy of the Humanities. Her books include *The Ecological Self* (1991), *Ecology and Democracy* (editor) (1996), *For Love of Matter: A Contemporary Panpsychism* (2003), *Journey to the Source of the Merri* (2003), *Reinhabiting Reality: Towards a Recovery of Culture* (2005), *Ardea: a philosophical novella* (2015) and *Without Animals Life is not Worth Living* (2015). She is the author of a hundred articles in the area of ecological philosophy and panpsychism. In addition to her research activities, she co-manages a private conservation reserve in Central Victoria.

Ben McKeown is an award-winning Indigenous artist of Wirangu and Kaurna, and non-Indigenous ancestries. He holds a Master of Visual Art and graduated valedictorian with a Master of Fine Art from the Victorian College of the Arts where he is currently engaged in a PhD research project. His approach is multi-disciplinary and conceptual, enabling him to explore ideas of histories, memories, identity and place, ideas often evidenced in his streetscape paintings. One of these evolved as a tapestry, now on permanent display at the State Library of Victoria, and woven at the Australian Tapestry Workshop. In 2018, he was featured in the documentary film *Can Art Stop a Bullet? William Kelly's Big Picture*. His works are held in the United Nations Collection (Geneva), State Library of Victoria (Vic.), National Gallery of Australia (ACT) and elsewhere.

Dr Ruth Mitchell is a paediatric neurosurgeon and cancer biologist living and working on unceded sovereign Aboriginal land. She is Co-Chair of the International Campaign to Abolish Nuclear Weapons (ICAN) Australia, and Chair of the Board of the International Physicians for the Prevention of Nuclear War (IPPNW). Born in Peru, and raised in Scotland, Ecuador and Canada, Ruth is passionate about diversity, inclusion, and the full participation of women and other underrepresented communities in the most important conversations of our time. Ruth has previously served as vice president of the Medical Association for the Prevention of War (MAPW).

Mick Pope has a PhD in meteorology from Monash University, and lectures in meteorology. He is currently completing a master's degree in theology, examining human responsibility in Genesis 1–3 and Anthropocene ethics. His books include *A Climate of Hope* with Claire Dawson, *A Climate of Justice*, and *All Things New*. He also hosts the podcast *The Natural Philosopher*.

Dianne Rayson is an ecotheologian who lectures at The University of Newcastle and Charles Sturt University and is an Adjunct Fellow of the Research Centre for Public and Contextual Theology (PaCT). Her research is in public theology for the Anthropocene and she is a scholar of Dietrich Bonhoeffer. Her recent book is *Bonhoeffer and Climate Change: Theology and Ethics for the Anthropocene* (Lexington 2021). As a public theologian she addresses contemporary social issues and ethical dilemmas such as war, rape culture, and public policy. She lives and works across Biripi and Awabakal country, between the mountains and the sea.

Omar Sakr is an award-winning poet born in Western Sydney to Lebanese and Turkish Muslim migrants. He is the author of *These Wild Houses* (Cordite 2017), and *The Lost Arabs* (UQP 2019), which won the 2020 Prime Minister's Literary Award for Poetry. *The Lost Arabs* was also shortlisted for the Judith Wright Calanthe Award, the John Bray Poetry Award, the NSW Premier's Multicultural Literary Award, and the Colin Roderick Award. It is released in the US and worldwide through Andrews McMeel Universal.

Anna Sakurai is a peripatetic artist and thinker from Tokyo and Melbourne whose curiosity has taken her to distant shores. After reading Philosophy, Politics and Economics (PPE) at Oxford University, she lived in Rome, where she worked for the United Nations. More recently, she has been a fellow at the European University Institute, where she investigated how social change can, and must, be upheld by building socially equitable and sustainable economies, one service, one product, one business at a time. Anna is co-founder of the Pacific Fellowship which funds good works throughout the Pacific.

Craig Santos Perez is an indigenous Chamoru writer from the Pacific Island of Guam. He is the author of five books of poetry and the co-editor of five anthologies. He is a professor of English at the University of Hawaii, Manoa.

Alex Skovron is the author of six poetry collections, most recently *Towards the Equator: New & Selected Poems* (2014) which was shortlisted in the Prime Minister's Literary Awards. Other publications include his prose novella *The Poet* (2005), and a book of short stories, *The Man who Took to his Bed* (2017). Alex's work has been translated into several languages, and his numerous public readings include appearances in China, Serbia, India, Ireland, Macedonia and Portugal. A new collection, *Letters from the Periphery*, is forthcoming. He was born in Poland, lived briefly in Israel, and arrived in Australia aged nine.

Deborah Storie previously lived in the lands now called Afghanistan where she worked in rural community development, disaster preparedness, and peace-building projects, and in leadership roles with an International Non-Government Organisation. She has evaluated community projects in Afghanistan, Asia, Africa and Australia, served on the Board of TEAR Australia, and participated in the Australian Council for International Development's Afghanistan Advisory Committee and the International Relations Stream of the Australia 2020 Summit (2008). Deborah now lives on the lands of the Wurundjeri people, works as a Baptist Pastor, and lectures in Biblical Studies at Stirling Theological College. She is an Honorary Research Associate at Whitley College, University of Divinity.

Kanchana Weerakoon founded Eco-Friendly Volunteers (https://www.eco-v.org/), which has organised leadership training campaigns on climate change and sustainability for young people in Sri Lanka. She is also past president of Australian-based Journeys for Climate Justice (https://www.journeysforclimatejustice.org.au/), and cofounded Edible Routes Foundation in New Delhi where she now lives. She works as a consultant on environmental sustainability in the South Asia region.

Asmi Wood is a professor of law and Sub-Dean (Indigenous) at the Australian National University (ANU) Law School. Most recently before that he was the Interim Director of the National Centre for Indigenous Studies (also at the ANU). His PhD was in the area of International Humanitarian Law (IHL), examining how law can be used to moderate the use of force by non-state actors.

_____

Acknowledgments

On a cool morning in early March 2021, I am writing from my home office on Boonwurrung (also spelt Bunurong) Country in bayside Melbourne. I acknowledge Boonwurrung land, seas and skies, and pay my respects to the elders, past, present and emerging, to Indigenous peoples contributing to this volume and to the lands, waters and skies of all the places from which this volume emerges and toward which it extends.

It is important that the first essay concerns the Treaty process in the state of Victoria and the centrality of truth-telling to that process. The essay is a transcript of a speech given last year by Jason Kelly, a Mutti Mutti, Wamba Wamba man, community elected member for the First Peoples' Assembly for the North West of Victoria. I am grateful to Jason for permission to reproduce his speech in this collection and to Vicki Clark and Sherry Balcombe for putting us in contact.

Thank you to all the contributors for their work. In particular, I acknowledge artists William Kelly and Benjamin McKeown and poets Alex Skovron, Andy Jackson, Bella Li and Susan Fealy, for permission to reproduce their works here. Thank you to Freya Mathews and Garry Worete Deverell for permission to include their invocational prayer-poems, to Julian Meehan and Deborah Hart for permission to reproduce the photo 'Climate Guardians Defending Westernport Bay against AGL's Ecocidal Gas Proposal, February 2021' and to Pauline Brightling for permission to include her photo 'Hallway and Street'. Thank you to Kanchana Weerakoon for the photos of Newton, Dhanushka and Chapa, and to these three young people for permission to share their stories. Thank you to the people whose experiences lie behind the vignettes in the essays by Mónica Maher and Deborah Storie, and for permission to tell their stories.

Particular thanks to Craig Santos Perez for permission to reproduce the poem 'Nuclear Family', which originally appeared in Craig Santos Perez, *Habitat Threshold* (Oakland, CA: Omnidawn, 2020, pp. 63–65), to Omar Sakr and University of Queensland Press for permission to reproduce the poem, 'Do Not Rush', which originally appeared in Omar Sakr, *The Lost Arabs* (St Lucia, QLD: UQP, 2019, pp. 50–51), and to Rose Lucas for permission to reproduce the poem, 'Streets of My Isolation', which originally appeared in Rose Lucas and Sharon Monagle, *2020 Shelter in Place: A Year in Poetry and Paint* (Seddon, Vic: Liquid Amber Press, 2021, pp. 39–40).

Finally, for their support of the project and this book, I thank Dr Jenny Grounds and Medical Association for the Prevention of War, Joseph Camilleri, Deborah Guess and the Toward a Just and Ecologically Sustainable Peace (JESP) team, and the University of Divinity, in particular the Network for Religion and Social Policy (formerly the Centre for Research in Religion and Social Policy), Pilgrim College and Trinity College Theological School. Many other bodies sponsored the JESP project, financially or in kind, including Australian Association for the Study of Religions, Australian Research Theology Foundation Inc., Borderlands Co-operative, Islamic Council of Victoria, Religions for Peace, Social Policy Connections, Society of Friends, Victorian Council of Churches, and many religious orders, as part of the JESP network. For funding in support of this book, I acknowledge with gratitude this broad network, as well as Pax Christi and University of Divinity. I offer my appreciation to the publishers Palaver Press, particularly Sally Gardner for her advice on the manuscript and Ian Robertson for the layout and typesetting.

My personal thanks to my partner Greg Price, and our sons Matthew and Andrew Elvey Price, for their ongoing encouragement and companionship.

— Anne Elvey

_____

A Just and Ecologically Sustainable Peace

In 2014, biblical scholar Keith Dyer, ecotheologian Deborah Guess and I initiated a research project, titled Ecological Aspects of War. While others had considered the implications of war for Earth and its ecosystems,[1] our focus was on religious, theological and biblical perspectives, although not necessarily as confessional or faith-based approaches to the intersections of war, peace, ecology and religion. Under the auspices of the Yarra Institute for Religion and Social Policy (YIRSP) and with support from University of Divinity, in 2015 the project team organised a conference, Ecological Aspects of War, from which two scholarly book publications emerged.[2] By 2017, YIRSP had handed over its work to the newly formed Centre for Research in Religion and Social Policy (RASP) at the University of Divinity. In conjunction with RASP, the project team planned two evening seminars in 2017. The first was The Legacy of War: Ecojustice Perspectives on Australia's Involvement in the Middle East, with guest speaker Deborah Storie who focused on Afghanistan and has an essay in this book. Taking as prompt Clive Hamilton's *Defiant Earth*, the second was titled Responding to the Anthropocene: What does it mean to be human responding to a deep future? and featured David Horrell from the UK, a leader in the Exeter-based Uses of the Bible in Environmental Ethics research project, and Jonathan Keren-Black from Australian Religious Response to Climate Change.[3] The Ecological Aspects of War project, in conjunction with an earlier ecotheological and religious studies project I worked on with David Gormley-O'Brien, Climate Change — Cultural Change, aimed to put ecological thinking at the fore of our thinking about justice and peace, and to affirm intersections between activism and scholarship.[4]

Encouraged by Joseph Camilleri, in 2018 Pax Christi and RASP collaborated to further this research — as activist scholarship — in a new project: Toward a Just and Ecologically Sustainable Peace (JESP). Between the Easter long weekend and Anzac Day, in April 2019 the JESP project held a major two-day conference, Earth at Peace, involving Indigenous speakers, including Bruce Pascoe and Naomi Wolfe, scholars of ecological feminist theology and peace building, for example Heather Eaton and Kevin Clements, nonviolence activists like Marie Dennis who has an essay in this volume, environmental philosophers like Freya Mathews who contributes a poetic invocation to this book, and many more. A public forum included Behrouz Boochani, a Kurdish journalist, then a refugee in offshore detention under the Australian Government's cruel asylum-seeker policies; he spoke by video link from Papua New Guinea.[5] A collection of scholarly essays from the conference was published as *Towards a Just and Ecologically Sustainable Peace: Navigating the Great Transition*.[6] The current book *Cloud Climbers: Declarations through Images and Words for a Just and Ecologically Sustainable Peace* is a companion to that volume and reflects another aspect of the project.

As Joseph Camilleri and Deborah Guess write in their preface to *Towards a Just and Ecologically Peace*, the 2019 conference 'had the usual components of a conference program (with keynote presentations and a number of panels) but also more dynamic aspects'.[7] These included working groups, a hypothetical, and an art exhibition and Anzac Eve cultural event, with an 'emphasis on linking thought, action, poetry and art'.[8] The aim was to enact collaborative possibilities across arts, activism and scholarship. This book records and responds to that impulse.

Collaboration

In partnership with the Earth at Peace conference, Christina Rowntree curated an exhibition of work by peace artist William Kelly, entitled 'Just Art', at Centre for Theology and Ministry in Parkville. The final evening of the conference was April 24, Anzac Eve, and in collaboration with Medical Association for the Prevention of War (MAPW), the conference closed with a celebration of art, music, poetry and speeches, which was both the official opening of the 'Just Art' exhibition and, in an MAPW tradition, offered a model of cooperation and inspiration across the arts as an alternative to the many commemorations of war the following day (ANZAC Day). MAPW representative Dr Jenny Grounds emceed the evening and Dr Ruth Mitchell, who is represented in this volume, spoke of her experience as an activist doctor. A local community choir The Brunswick Rogues sang with abandon, Celtic harpist Cath Connelly played movingly, and five poets read their work.

Months earlier, by invitation of the JESP organising committee, these five poets — Alex Skovron, Andy Jackson, Bella Li, Susan Fealy and myself — agreed with William Kelly to respond to his work. Generously, Bill trusted each of us to take home a work or works to which we would respond with an ekphrastic poem. Our poems were mounted beside the works for the exhibition. The six works by William Kelly—*Tender Dreams / Tentative Futures II*, *Dreams on a Flag*, *Childhoods*, *The Arrival*, *Dialogue II: Religion*, and *Witness / Cloud Climbers II*—and the accompanying five poems — '8193–II' (Bella Li), 'How Many Times Must I Send You into the World?' (Susan Fealy), 'Hands' (Alex Skovron), 'Face to Face' (Andy Jackson) and 'Where We Sleep' (Anne Elvey) — form the framework for this book. In addition, this book includes William Kelly's *Peace Not War/Bridge Builder*s, and two collaborative artworks by Benjamin McKeown and William Kelly, *Journeys and Destinations* and *Closing the Gap* which frame the text. Interspersed with these nine works are poems, including 'Nuclear Family' by Craig Santos Perez and 'Do Not Rush' by Omar Sakr, short essays, reflections and invocations, all oriented toward a just and ecologically sustainable peace.

This book reflects the conviction that the arts, literature, activism and scholarship can together contribute to the kinds of cultural shift requisite for a peace that flows from and extends to human relations with the natural world. The contributors are artists, poets, activists, ecological, feminist, legal, theological and religious scholars; their tone is often urgent and passionate, as if they are creating a manifesto. Their artworks and writings, poetic and scholarly, are declarations for a just and ecologically sustainable peace; they attest that creative and scholarly works can function as forms of, and accompaniments to, activism.

William Kelly: Art and Activism

William Kelly's work is emblematic of this nexus between the arts and activism. Janet McKenzie comments on the centrality of 'social commitment' to Kelly's work, the way ethics and aesthetics are enmeshed in his artistic practice.[9] Just a few weeks before the first COVID-19 lockdown in Melbourne in 2020, I was fortunate to see the feature film, *Can Art Stop a Bullet? William Kelly's Big Picture*. This film traces the collaborative nature of Kelly's work, its commemorations of the violence of war and state-based oppression, his engagements in resistance to war, from Guernica to Vietnam, protest at US imperialism, and critique of British colonisation's ongoing impacts across First Nations Country in what is now called Australia. His work does not turn from the trauma to which it bears witness, but in the midst of social and ecological distress Kelly's art opens toward hope for different 'tentative futures' in the 'tender dreams' of peace and flourishing for generations to come. In the context of the JESP project these generations are not only human, but extend to all beings under the strain of environmental destruction in its many forms.

Speaking out

Since World War II in Australia, questions of war and peace, social justice and responses to heightening ecological destruction and trauma, have intersected in activist movements for nuclear disarmament, conscientious objection to wars, most notably the Vietnam War, movements for Aboriginal Rights, the rights of women, and for environmental protection, in recent times focused around climate change. While many of these movements took off in the 1960s and seemed to be at a height in the 1970s and 1980s, they have continued into the twenty-first century with younger generations taking a lead, for example, in the School Strike 4 Climate and Black Lives Matter movements. At the same time, there is growing awareness of the partiality of western liberal underpinnings of some earlier activist undertakings and a broader understanding of the need to recognise the multidimensional and intersectional character of violence, oppression, protest and resistance, and most crucially to take leadership from First Nations. This collection is a small contribution to that complex space of contemporary thinking and activism for a just and ecologically sustainable peace.

Reflecting the beginnings of the JESP project as a collaboration between Pax Christi and the University of Divinity network for Research in Religion and Social Policy, a number of the essays here express faith-based responses, including Christians who write with an ear both to the colonial legacies of Christianity and their traditions' resources for peace and ecological integrity. There are also contributions from First Nations, as well from activist-scholars with experience in Afghanistan, Central and South America, and from practitioners in local and international ecological and peace movements. I was surprised on receiving them that more essays than I expected reference Christian or biblical belief, in the context of peace, nonviolence and ecological justice. Biblical texts themselves and the legacy of biblical religions are at best ambiguous in relation to violence. For many of us with roots in biblical religious traditions, the recent 2017 Report of the Australian Royal Commission into Institutional Responses to Child Sexual Abuse shows that violent abuse of children (and we could add vulnerable adults), can occur alongside institutional moves toward decolonisation, peace and justice, sometimes in the same schools, churches and monasteries. At the same time, patriarchal attitudes and systems remain entrenched in many, but not all, institutional religions. On a different scale, in our daily lives as artists, writers and activists, our economic reliance on and unwilling (but nonetheless real) entanglement with global networks of fossil fuel production and trade, trafficking in people, reliance on underpaid workers in unsafe occupational situations, and the impacts on other species of the ways many of us consume, mean that social and environmental oppressions contaminate our nonviolent aspirations and practices. Nothing is pure.

This book does not aim for purity in the midst of the complex entanglements of planetary life and global economics, but offers a series of voices, in images and words, calling forth resistances and alternatives in this mess/ mesh, 'staying with the trouble', as Donna Haraway recommends.[10] For the 'disturbing times' in which we live, writes Haraway, our 'task is to become capable, with each other in all of our bumptious kinds, of response'.[11] This requires 'inventive connection', quiet retreat, engaging in presence as 'mortal' beings enmeshed in multiple 'unfinished configurations of places, times, matters, meanings'.[12] This book in a small way is one such material place of engagement: inventive, connecting and ultimately unfinished.

The book opens with Benjamin McKeown and William Kelly's artwork, *Journeys and Destinations*; centred around a mother and child under the southern cross, are two hands, one white and one black, and two birds, one caged and one free. The linocut was made for the United Nations 50th Anniversary of the Universal Declaration of Human Rights. While Australia contributed to the formation of and is a signatory to the Universal Declaration of Human Rights, it was one of four nations that in 2007 voted against the United Nations Declaration on the Rights of Indigenous Peoples.

Jason Kelly is a Mutti Mutti, Wamba Wamba man, and community elected member for the First Peoples' Assembly for the North West of Victoria. Following *Journeys and Destinations,* is an edited transcript of a speech by Kelly given in November 2020 on the necessity for truth-telling to be part of the Treaty process in Victoria. Since then, The Victorian Truth and Justice Commission was announced in March 2021. For Kelly, an understanding of the United Nations Declaration on the Rights of Indigenous Peoples is vital for this truth-telling process.

Truth-telling is a form of reparative story-telling and listening. In his essay focusing on the multiple meanings, in Maori, Samoan and Tongan, of the word *ao* (cloud), Jione Havea, a biblical scholar and native pastor of the Methodist Church in Tonga, currently living in Melbourne, enacts a form of *talanoa* (story-weaving). This story-weaving is a gift toward peace that tells the truth about ongoing colonisation in the Pacific. Following Havea's essay, is the poem 'Nuclear Family' by Craig Santos Perez, an indigenous Chamoru writer from the Pacific Island of Guam, working in Hawaii. The poem weaves a powerful story of Indigenous ancestry and nuclear fallout. Then follows Omar Sakr's 'Do Not Rush' which details the violent legacy of US militarism on predominantly Arab and Muslim nations in what is sometimes called the Middle East. The poem asks poignantly: what if it took as long to kill as to gestate a person?

Two artworks by William Kelly then accompany Bella Li's poem '8193-II': *Tender Dreams/Tentative Futures* and *Dreams on a Flag.* The poem, responding to both works, addresses colonisation and colony collapse in our time, rephrasing a quote from a message carried in the exploratory craft, Voyager, launched from Earth into space in 1977: 'This is a present from a small, distant world ... We are attempting to survive our time so we may live into yours'.[13] What might enable our survival as a planetary community, and not as humans alone? The next two essays come from long time leaders in the Pax Christi movement. Joseph Camilleri focuses on the potential of dialogue between cultures, religions and civilisations toward a just and ecologically sustainable peace. Marie Dennis argues for a Roman Catholic commitment to education in nonviolence across the globe. Rabbi Jonathan Keren-Black, a founding member of the Jewish Ecological Coalition, maintains that equality of opportunity is essential if work toward a just and ecologically sustainable peace is to succeed.

Where the artworks *Tender Dreams/Tentative Futures* and *Dreams on a Flag* reference children and the determination that we must not pass on present violence, the title of the next work *Childhoods* is more specific. In this work, William Kelly uses another maternal image — the connectedness of mother and child while breastfeeding — and surrounds this with a series of references to childhoods under shadow and at play. Susan Fealy's poem

'How Many Times Must I Send You into the World?' creates its own series of vignettes in response, asking what kinds of world we are creating for children to negotiate. The following essay by Dr Ruth Mitchell, a neurosurgeon, combines her medical work with her anti-nuclear and peace activism; both require close listening and witness to the stories, those of her patients and those of survivors of nuclear weapons, such as Setsuko Thurlow who was twelve when the atomic bomb dropped on her home town of Hiroshima. Deborah Storie's essay arises from her familiarity with a site of more recent conflict, Afghanistan, where she lived and worked as a guest with local peoples for several years. Her essay titled 'We long for peace, but not any peace' captures in vignettes the voices of the people she knew, demonstrating the complex outcomes of Australia's involvement in the war in Afghanistan, and the predictable failures to fulfil its aims. Drawing on ethicist Margaret Somerville, Storie asks if Australia's intervention in Afghanistan might stem from a societal failure to exercise an 'empathetic imagination'.

Two hands tied with a pleated cord form the next work, *The Arrival* by William Kelly, to which Alex Skovron responds with a poem of many questions, 'Hands', asking if our hearts are wanting, our hands tied. The essay which follows, 'The Cord' by Deborah Guess, answers both the artwork and the poem, arguing that recognising the entanglements of climate change with consumerism, we might adopt a voluntary self-limiting, symbolised in hands tied with a soft cord. Mick Pope, a meteorologist and ecotheologian, writes of kenosis, a self-emptying, in the context of anthropogenic climate change. Ecotheologian and Bonhoeffer scholar, Dianne Rayson writes from first-hand experience of the 2019–2020 catastrophic bushfire season in Eastern Australia. Reflecting on grief at the deaths of so many other creatures, she sees Christian hope symbolised in the resurrection as arriving in the return of breathable air, regeneration of forests and collective resistance to further destruction. Anna Sakurai reflects on the need to listen to First Nations' wisdom on fire management and care for Country.

William Kelly's *Peace, Not War / Bridge Builders* resonates with these calls to hopeful action, and forms a transition to three essays addressing the urgency of ecological justice in the framework of feminist liberation theology. The essays by Anne Elvey, Wanda Deifelt and Mónica Maher arise from papers presented to the Feminist Liberation Theology Network in the US in November 2019 and November 2020. From Australia, Elvey argues for foregrounding the epistemologies, experience and sovereignty of First Nations in action addressing climate change. From her experience in Brazil, Deifelt adopts an intersectional approach, describing colonial and neo-colonial impacts of climate change for Indigenous peoples in the Amazon, and proposing a mode of response, *buen vivir*, that holds together human dignity and the wellbeing of all creation. Based in Ecuador, Maher tells stories from feminist theologians, in Mexico and Honduras, of compassion exercised *in extremis* during the combined crises of Hurricane Eta and COVID-19 in 2020. Maher reimagines salvation in terms of tenderness and *corazonar*, 'thinking with the heart'.

Dialogue II: Religion by William Kelly draws on predominantly Christian symbolism in a grave response to oppressive violence. Andy Jackson's poem 'Face to Face' answers with reference to the Hoddle St mass shootings in 1987, and a nearby statue of St John the Baptist in Clifton Hill. This violence for the poet is in a lineage of colonial violence on Wurundjeri Country. The poem closes with the poet 'speechless and ashamed'. Asmi Wood in his essay 'Human Voices' addresses global systems that work to keep us 'speechless' and argues for the use of 'international legal mechanisms' to hear and 'protect the collective voices of ordinary people'. Creative activist, Deborah Hart, in her essay 'Choices' makes a passionate call to action — to choose life for our planetary community. Kanchana Weerakoon and Jim Crosthwaite describe an ongoing activist project they initiated with young people in Sri Lanka which creates social bonds for peace and ecological wholeness, funded by climate change offsets.

The final section of the book opens with William Kelly's *Witness / Cloud Climbers II,* followed by Anne Elvey's ekphrastic poem 'Where We Sleep', which moves toward 'another way of ground'. Three works of poetry and invocation come next. Rose Lucas captures a moment in COVID-19 lockdown when in her local neighbourhood people connected across distance through gesture rather than proximity or touch. Freya Mathews, in a poetic invocation, calls for a sacred attentiveness to place: 'Let the Mountain Be Your Temple'. Trawloolway man and theologian Garry Worete Deverell, offers a prayer to be used by settler churches in the face of the ongoing colonisation of Country and the ecological catastrophe that has accompanied invasion.

I have wondered about finishing the text of the book with this Christian prayer, its focus on repentance, its appeal to a religion that arrived with the colonisers. But this collection of art, poetry and prose witnesses repeatedly to 'staying with the trouble', to hope and truth in the face of unfinished business, when we do not always have an answer to where to turn, a question posed by Deverell's prayer. While I might have included a response essay or an afterword, in the spirit of affirming artwork as voice, the book's response and afterword is the collaborative work, *Closing the Gap* by Benjamin McKeown and William Kelly.

This collection is selective rather than comprehensive. As such I hope it creates spaces for ongoing nonviolent creative and activist undoings of the multiple violences of racism, sexism, misogyny, classism, speciesism, and the lived horrors these entail. The 2019–2020 Australian bushfires and the current COVID-19 pandemic echo across many of the contributions, as does a wider feminist engagement with Earth under threat of continuing anthropocentric and patriarchal violence. In the midst of intergenerational, transnational and interspecies trauma, I entrust this collection to readers in hope.

1. For example, Jurgen Brauer, *War and Nature: The Environmental Consequences of War in a Globalized World* (Lanham, MD: Altamira Press, 2009).

2. Anne Elvey and Keith Dyer, with Deborah Guess (eds), *Ecological Aspects of War: Engagements with Biblical Texts* (London: Bloomsbury T&T Clark, 2017); Anne Elvey, Deborah Guess and Keith Dyer (eds), *Ecological Aspects of War: Religious and Theological Perspectives* (*A Forum for Theology in the World* 3, no. 2; Adelaide: ATF Press, 2016).

3. Clive Hamilton, *Defiant Earth: The Fate of Humans in the Anthropocene* (Sydney: Allen & Unwin, 2017).

4. From the Climate Change—Cultural Change project, the following volume appeared: Anne Elvey and David Gormley-O'Brien (eds), *Climate Change—Cultural Change: Religious Responses and Responsibilities* (Preston, Vic.: Mosaic Books, 2013).

5. Behrouz Boochani's award winning book from that time is *No Friend but the Mountains: Writing from Manus Prison* (trans. Omid Tofighian; Sydney: Picador, 2018).

6. Joseph Camilleri and Deborah Guess (eds), *Towards a Just and Ecologically Sustainable Peace: Navigating the Great Transition* (Singapore: Palgrave Macmillan, 2020).

7. Joseph Camilleri and Deborah Guess, 'Preface', in *Towards a Just and Ecologically Sustainable Peace*, vi.

8. Camilleri and Guess, 'Preface', vi.

9. Janet McKenzie, 'William Kelly, Artist as Peacemaker', *Studio International* (15 August 2008), https://www.studiointernational.com/index.php/william-kelly---artist-as-peacemaker (accessed 13 April 2021).

10. Donna Haraway, *Staying with the Trouble: Making Kin in the Chthulucene* (Durham: Duke University Press, 2016).

11. Haraway, *Staying with the Trouble*, 1.

12. Haraway, *Staying with the Trouble*, 1.

13. 'Howdy Strangers/Voyager Golden Record', NASA, https://www.nasa.gov/missions/deepspace/MI_CM_Feature_02.html (accessed 15 April 2021).

Benjamin McKeown & William Kelly **Journeys and Destinations**
2010, digital print on archival paper, 29.5 x 21 cm.

The First Peoples' Assembly of Victoria has successfully called on the Victorian Government to support a truth-telling process. Truth-telling is a process of openly sharing historical truths after periods of conflict. They acknowledge past wrongs, ensure an accurate historical record and set a common understanding of our shared history.

The Assembly is working now to design a truth-telling process in Victoria that is guided by and reflects the needs of community. We believe that truth-telling will lay the necessary groundwork for successful Treaties.[2]

My name is Jason Kelly. I'm a Mutti Mutti, Wamba Wamba man, community elected member for the First Peoples' Assembly for the North West of Victoria. I'm the author of the resolution regarding the truth-telling. By no means is it only my idea. First and foremost, I want to pay my respects and to acknowledge everyone's work that went into it beforehand and led up to this, all the founders of our ACCOs (Aboriginal Controlled Community Organisations), our Tent Embassies, all of our human rights activists, all of those who were in the struggle right from the beginning, those who, back to the Commonwealth Games in Brisbane, were protesting then, all the marches, all the activism that led up to this; this is all part of that.

For me, truth-telling has always been at the front of everything in my life-time (I was born in 1972), everything I participated in. Every time we've had marches: we've been marching for truth as long as we've been marching for land rights, as long as we've been marching for Treaty. It's not a new concept. It's something we've actively campaigned for at a local level, state level, and a national level. I go back and think of the first opening of the Federal Parliament and an old Wiradjuri Uncle Jimmy Clements on his own turned up to the Parliament there in Canberra and made it clear that he was there to assert his rights as a sovereign owner of the Federation. I think of everyone else who has come since then: William Cooper, Jack Patten, the birth of our ACCOs that were born under a human rights agenda. All of this, all ties in. It is all part of this accumulation of where we are now with the truth-telling.[3]

For me personally there was only one day, yesterday, on 17 November 2017 we brought Mungo Man home on Country. I was one of the speakers then with my auntie, Aunty Tookie, and I made it clear then at Mungo about the importance of the truth-telling and of the rest of Australia needing to have an understanding of that truth.

So then coming back to Victoria and with the Government committing to a Treaty, I felt that it was really important that whilst as an assembly we are responsible for establishing a framework, it is really essential and really important that we have to have the truth-telling so that we can have a human rights focus. We can have an inquiry, a commission, whatever it's going to be called, with a human rights focus, less the evidential facts and findings, so that it makes it easier when it comes to Treaty, when it comes to negotiations stages of the Treaty.

But I'm really mindful, really aware of the distrust, and the Minister herself always talks about the trust deficit.[4] We know that better than anyone as Aboriginal people. There is a trust deficit. I wanted to be sure when I put the resolution up. None of us are comfortable having these things assessed under Australian law or Victorian law, because Australian and Victorian law has inflicted and continues to inflict human rights abuses on Aboriginal people.

So, when I put the resolution up, there were a couple of things in there, the preamble for advancing the Treaty process with Aboriginal Victorians. It's actually in the legislation, mentioning the truth, or something that ensures all Victorians are included in it. I wanted to ensure that we had the United Nations Declaration of the Rights of Indigenous Peoples as part of the resolution. And international best practice in the use of comparable truth and justice inquiries and principles of truth and transitional justice-based procedures. This is a new concept on the world stage, probably in the last 30 or so years. Going back to the international best practices I looked at a lot of things. I know that there have been 40 different countries that have had truth enquiries. Mauritius was one example that had an independent one and they went back 370 years to investigate the impacts of slavery and the economic consequences of it since then.

The good news was that at Assembly we all got together and we passed this resolution. The good thing about that also was that the Government was really quick to respond. The Minister took it to cabinet and got cabinet approval. The Minister took the resolution in its raw form and so cabinet have agreed to the resolution for the points I just spoke out about.

The reason I put the international best practices was because, when you are looking at it, I wanted this to be a public education thing with a focus on victims and survivors first and foremost. But when we look at the marches, look at the Black Lives Matter rallies that we've had, when we look at the Invasion Day marches, the number of Australian youth who are marching with us, we're turning out 50,000, we're turning out 100,000 people. These are non-Aboriginal Australians that are demanding a right to truth. They are demanding a right to truth. They are marching in solidarity with us.

So, in a way if the government is going to be committing to a Treaty, we talk about free, informed and prior consent, it is an important tool to also give free, informed and prior consent to the rest of Victoria as to why. Let them have a clear understanding as to why we have committed to a Treaty and why the Victorian Government is committed to a Treaty on their behalf. Then for me it is just about seeing the potential when we are doing community engagement as running parallel with public education, because I think that for us now it is an opportunity for all Victorian Aboriginal people to have an understanding of what is the United Nations Declaration of Rights of Indigenous Peoples, what is International Law, also when you look at the International Convention on the Prevention and Punishment of the Crime of Genocide, there were four elements there that 100% tick all the boxes, when you are looking at the Massacre maps, when you are looking at the Royal Commission into Deaths in Custody, when you are looking at the *Bringing Them Home* report.[5] It is also an opportunity for the Government now to come out and stipulate under the lens of International Law that the Government has committed genocide on Aboriginal people.

It's also an avenue, if you look on the international law scope, customary international law is where Aboriginal Law is recognised at an international level, but it's not so much about prosecution for stuff 200 years ago. It's about putting the government on trial and having a finding of genocide. It's about a right to know for everyone else. It needs to be a really important public education campaign running alongside, parallel with Treaty. The rest of Victoria needs to have a crystal-clear understanding of what history has done to us, but how we have found the answers for ourselves also. In a cultural context, it's like having the smoking ceremony for us; the truth-telling findings in the commission is the spear that Victoria has to take. So, we're spearing Victoria in the leg, but also after we deliver that spear, we're responsible to all heal together. Essentially that's pretty much the basis of what I see as a critical element of truth-telling and Treaty.

1. Edited transcript of presentation by Jason Kelly as part of Truth-telling livestream discussion, Facebook, 18 November 2020, https://www.facebook.com/firstpeoplesvic/videos/964888533919204 (accessed 21 December 2020).
2. First Peoples' Assembly of Victoria, https://www.firstpeoplesvic.org/our-work/truth-telling/ (accessed 21 December 2020).
3. Since this speech was given, The Victorian Truth and Justice Commission has been announced; see Sumeyya Ilanbey and Paul Sakkal, '"Please hear our voices": Truth and justice commission announced', *The Age* (9 March 2021), https://www.theage.com.au/politics/victoria/please-hear-our-voices-truth-and-justice-commission-announced-20210309-p5792v.html (accessed 24 March 2021).
4. 'The Minister' refers to The Victorian State Government Minister for Aboriginal Affairs, Gabrielle Williams MP. See her 'Message from the Minister' in relation to Advancing the Victorian Treaty Process, Annual Report 2019–20, https://www.aboriginalvictoria.vic.gov.au/advancing-victorian-treaty-process-annual-report-2019-20/message-minister (accessed 11 January 2021).
5. One source for Massacre maps is the Colonial Frontier Massacres research project, University of Newcastle, https://c21ch.newcastle.edu.au/colonialmassacres/map.php (accessed 11 January 2021). The final report of the Royal Commission investigating Aboriginal Deaths in Custody was signed 15 April 1991, and made 339 recommendations: 'Recommendations of the Royal Commission into Aboriginal Deaths in Custody', Aboriginal Legal Rights Movement, http://www.alrm.org.au/wp-content/uploads/2015/05/Royal-Commission-into-Aboriginal-Deaths-in-Custody-1.pdf (accessed 11 January 2021). The *Bringing Them Home* report can be accessed online at: *Bringing Them Home: Report of the National Inquiry into the Separation of Aboriginal and Torres Strait Islander Children from Their Families* (Commonwealth of Australia 1997), https://www.humanrights.gov.au/sites/default/files/content/pdf/social_justice/bringing_them_home_report.pdf (accessed 11 January 2021).

Further Reading
— Advancing the Treaty Process with Aboriginal Victorians Act 2018. Authorised Version No. 001, 1 August 2018, https://content.legislation.vic.gov.au/sites/default/files/50f587e2-f753-3e01-b2ca-2f86930eef93_18-28aa001%20authorised.pdf (accessed 11 January 2021).
— Dunstan, Joseph. 'What Australia's first Aboriginal truth and justice commission might look like',

ABC News, 12 December 2020, https://www.abc.net.au/news/2020-12-12/australian-aboriginal-truth-and-justice-commission-what-is-it/12956326 (accessed 11 January 2021).

— First Peoples' Assembly of Victoria, https://www.firstpeoplesvic.org/ (accessed 11 January 2021).

— Treaty in Victoria. Aboriginal Victoria, https://www.aboriginalvictoria.vic.gov.au/treaty (accessed 11 January 2021).

— Truth and Justice Commission (Mauritius). *Report of the Truth and Justice Commission*, Volume 1, November 2011, https://reparations.qub.ac.uk/assets/uploads/2009-2011-Mauritius-Truth-Commission.pdf (accessed 11 January 2021).

— United Nations. *United Nations Declaration of the Rights of Indigenous Peoples*. Resolution adopted by the General Assembly on 13 September 2007, https://www.un.org/development/desa/indigenouspeoples/wp-content/uploads/sites/19/2018/11/UNDRIP_E_web.pdf (accessed 11 January 2021).

— United Nations. *Convention on the Prevention and Punishment of the Crime of Genocide* (Genocide Convention), https://www.un.org/en/genocideprevention/genocide-convention.shtml (accessed 11 January 2021).

———————

Hine-te-aparangi sighted a long body of cloud over the horizon and called out, 'He ao! He ao!' (a cloud, a cloud). With her husband Kupe, they discerned that land must be under the cloud. So, they directed their *waka hourua* (voyaging canoe) to the cloud and, as they hoped, they found whenua (land) under the *ao*/cloud.[1]

Hine-te-aparangi[2] and Kupe are remembered as the first native Māori family to land on the group of islands that were later called Aotearoa (*ao*/cloud-*tea*/white-*roa*/long), affectionately called as the '[land of the] long white cloud'. After sighting (by Abel Tasman in 1642 and James Cook in 1762), invasion, settlement and colonisation by Europeans, the Aotearoa islands also became known as New Zealand (for 'new sea land').

Over land, *ao*/cloud attracts hope for rain. In the moana (sea), *ao*/cloud feeds the longing for whenua (land). In both contexts, *ao*/cloud is in the sky above, but under the sun, the moon and the stars.

ao/overseer

In Te Reo Māori (Māori language), the term *ao* carries other meanings that are shared with other native tongues in the region. With Gagana Samoa (Samoan language), for instance, *ao* also refers to having oversight. In this connection, *ao o Samoa* is the title for Samoa's head of state.

As *ao*/cloud is in the sky, so is *ao*/overseer in the community. The *ao*/overseer navigates the community along the rhythms of whenua (land) and moana (sea), and along the lines drawn by native customs and traditions. The customs and traditions are gifts that are passed on from one generation to another, similar to what Yolngu people in the north of Australia call 'raypirri'.[3]

In Pasifika (for Oceania, Pacific Islands), the rhythms of whenua and moana, and the lines drawn by customs and traditions, are impacted by the energies (another connotation of the term *ao*) of the sun, moon and stars above. Moreover, these 'visible' realms are also impacted by the hidden energies/*ao* in the underworld.

Put another way, effective *ao*/overseers guide their communities according to the *ao*/energies of life and living. The *ao*/overseers are therefore responsible, and they provide guidance and oversight, but they are not the sovereign authorities (in the imperial sense).

ao/pluck

In Lea FakaTonga (Tongan language), *ao* also refers to the practices of plucking and gathering flowers or fruits from the field or bush. When someone returns from the moana and, on the way home, plucks a flower to put in her hair or behind his ears — that practice is *ao kakala* (plucking flower/fragrance). Depending on the season, she or he may pluck enough for a *lei* (garland).

Along this line, the term *ao* also applies to the picking of fruits, from trees and from the ground, to eat on the way or to take home. A similar practice is done in the biblical story of Ruth. She went out one day to glean, and she ended up in the part of the field that belonged to Boaz. Ruth followed behind the harvesters, and what they dropped she picked up to take home — for herself and her mother-in-law. In this connection, the term *ao* may also apply to the practice of gleaning.

ao talanoa

The word *ao* means more than cloud in all three native languages. With due respect to native speakers in all three Pasifika languages, i bring a sample of the many and rich meanings of *ao* into this reflection to provide a frame for the following *ao talanoa* around sustainable peace. At this juncture, i offer a brief explanation of another native Pasifika term — *talanoa*.

The term talanoa carries three meanings: story, telling (of stories), conversation (around stories and telling events). First, the legend about Hine-te-aparangi and Kupe discovering Aotearoa is a talanoa. Second, my partial telling of that legend above is an event of talanoa (telling). There are other stories (talanoa) in the Māori legend, but my telling focused on the *ao*/cloud. In other words, my telling is selective and directed, and therefore skewed. Third, my weaving of *ao*/cloud with other meanings of the term *ao* is also talanoa (as storyweaving). Talanoa is both native custom (orality) as well as practice (oratory, presented above in writing), the intersection of which makes the practices of talanoa embody *ao*. Talanoa provides guidance (*ao*/overseer) as well as resources (*ao*/pluck) for this reflection on sustainable peace.

Taking *ao*/clouding as sign of hope that sustainable peace is possible (as in the expectation of whenua under the cloud), this *ao talanoa* suggests that sustainable peace could endure if sustainable *ao*/overseeing (rather than overtaking) and sustainable *ao*/plucking (rather than, metaphorically speaking, milking and mining whenua and moana) are practiced. I use *ao talanoa* in reference to practices in which peace is hoped, enabled, practiced and sustained. When those practices become habits,[4] they may be added to the customs and traditions that one generation could gift as *raypirri* to future generations. At the intersection of *ao talanoa* with *raypirri*, i close by highlighting two details.

First, sustainable peace is prevented and threatened when overseers (leaders, governments, missions) assume that they have sovereignty over whenua (land), moana (sea) and raypirri (customs and traditions). The confusion of *ao*/oversight with sovereignty (power, control, dominion) has contributed to the displacement, dispossession and disempowering of native peoples in Pasifika and Australia. Problems arise and multiply when natives think that they have conceded to *ao*/oversight by foreign authorities (including religions), but those authorities assume that they have been given dominion over native whenua, moana, people and raypirri.

Second, when the confusion described above leads to abuse of native people, whenua, moana, people and raypirri, *ao talanoa* may be rekindled to recover peace. This could take place in two steps: (1) the practices of *ao/*plucking may be performed to highlight details of the talanoa that are usually ignored — the ignoring of which leaves room for abuse to take place. I accordingly *ao/*plucked the Māori legend by favouring Hine-te-aparangi (as a woman) in the discovery of Aotearoa (before the Europeans). (2) Talanoa as storyweaving may be used as a tool for enriching the narratives that steer the relations between natives and abusive overseers. This second task is more than seeking to rewrite the 'master's narrative'; it also requires weaving native insights and native talanoa to the master's narrative. This second task is 'in progress' in the case of Aotearoa, but still lacking for first peoples of Australia, West Papua, Kanaky (New Caledonia), Ma'ohi Nui (French Polynesia), Rapa Nui (Easter Island), Tutuila (American Samoa), Hawai'i, Guam and the Northern Mariana Islands. Peace cannot be sustained in the waters of Pasifika and Australia, while these (is)lands are under occupation.

---

1. According to Māori legends, Kupe and Hine-te-aparangi came from Hawaiki in pursuit of *Wheke-a-Muturangi* (a giant octopus), but i leave that focus for another retelling. For this reflection, i focus on the significance of the *ao/*cloud.
2. Oral tradition identifies her as Kuramārōtini, the wife of Hoturapa, Kupe's friend whom he left to drown in the sea so that he could take his wife.
3. See Maratja Dhamarrandji with Jione Havea, 'Receive, Touch, Feel, and Give *Raypirri*', in *Indigenous Australia and the Unfinished Business of Theology: Cross-cultural Engagement*, ed. Jione Havea (New York: Palgrave, 2014), 9–15.
4. In *ao talanoa*, sustained practice is basic. As a parent to a seven-year-old daughter, this call for sustained practice is about maintaining routines.

Further Reading
— Dhamarrandji, Maratja with Jione Havea. 'Receive, Touch, Feel, and Give *Raypirri*.' In *Indigenous Australia and the Unfinished Business of Theology: Cross-cultural Engagement*, edited by Jione Havea, 9–15. New York: Palgrave, 2014.
— Havea, Jione. 'Diaspora Contexted: Talanoa, Reading, and Theologizing, as Migrants.' *Black Theology* 11, no. 2 (2013): 185–200.
— Havea, Jione. 'Islander Criticism: Waters, Ways, Worries.' In *Sea of Readings: The Bible in the South Pacific*, edited by Jione Havea, 1–20. Atlanta: SBL, 2018.
— Havea, Jione. 'The Vanua is Fo'ohake.' In *Black Marks on the White Page*, edited by Witi Ihimaera and Tina Makereti, 135–40. Auckland: Penguin Random House, 2017.

7

In the beginning, _____ and _____
stood on the bridge of heaven and stirred the sea
with a jeweled spear until the first island was born.
Then one day, men who claimed to be gods
said: "Let there be atomic light," and there was
a blinding flash, a mushroom cloud, and radiating
fire. "This will end all wars," they said,
"This will bring peace to the divided world."

6

In the beginning, _____ and _____
ascended from the First World of darkness
until they reached the glittering waters
of this Fourth World, where the yellow snake,
_____, dwelled underground.
Then one day, men who claimed to be gods
said: "Let there be uranium," and they dug
a thousand unventilated mines. They unleashed
_____ and said: "This will enrich us all."

5

In the beginning, _____ spoke the islands
into being and created four gods to protect
each direction. The first people emerged
from a wound in _____'s body.
Then one day, men who claimed to be gods
said: "Let there be thermonuclear light,"
and there were countless detonations. "Bravo!"
They exclaimed, "This is for the good of mankind."

4

In the beginning, _____ transformed
the eyes of _____ into the sun and moon,
and his back into an island. Then her body
transformed into stone and birthed my people.
Then one day, men who claimed to be gods
said: "Let there be a bone seeker," and trade winds
rained strontium 90 upon us, and irradiated ships
were washed in our waters. And they said:
"This is for national security."

3

In the beginning, _____ created earth from mud.
Then his younger brother, _____, carried
a woven basket full of the first people to the Great Basin.
Then one day, the men who claimed to be gods
said: "Let there be plowshares," and the desert
cratered, and white dust snowed upon the four corners.
And they said: "This is for peaceful construction."

2

"The militarization of light has been widely acknowledged as a
historical rupture that brought into being a continuous Nuclear Age,
but less understood is the way in which our bodies are written by these
wars of light."—Elizabeth DeLoughrey, "Radiation Ecologies and the
Wars of Light" (2009)

... /

Craig Santos Perez **Nuclear Family**

1

In the beginning, there was no contamination.
Then the men who claimed to be gods said:
"Let there be fallout," and our lands and waters
became proving grounds, waste dumps,
and tailings. "Let there be fallout," and there was
a chain reaction of leukemia, lymphoma,
miscarriages, birth defects, and cancer.
"Let there be fallout," and there's no half-life of
grief when a loved one dies from radiation disease,
there's no half-life of sorrow when our children
inherit this toxic legacy, this generational
and genetic aftermath, this fission of worlds.

0

Let there be the disarmament of the violent nucleus
within nations. Let there be a proliferation of justice
and peace across our atomic cartographies: from
Hiroshima and Nagasaki to the Marshall Islands.
From the Navajo and Shoshone Nations to Mororua,
Fangataufa, In Ekker, Kiritimati, Maralinga, Amchitka,
Malan, Montebello Islands, Malden Island, Pokhran,
Ras Koh Hills, Chagai District, Semipalatinsk,
Novaya Zemlya, Three Mile Island, Chernobyl,
Punggye-ri, and Fukushima. Let there be peace
and justice for the downwinders, from Utah
to Guam to every irradiated species.

———

to make a judgment.
You can savage a body at speed.
A city can be ruined in an hour.
A love of decades dashed in a second.
It takes nine months to start a life.
It should take as long to end one.
After a trigger is pulled and before
a bullet lands, give nine months
to the target to welcome the hole,
to accept the blood, the blunt lead,
the new body. I know it is possible
to allow a death to gestate. Watch
time mushroom out from a bomber
and seasons unfurl on the city below.
Spring in Baghdad to winter in Aleppo,
one final semester of learning, a retreat
by a river, time enough to be thankful
for old books and DVDs borrowed,
to study the bullet or the blast with
a lover's eye. It seems a short goodbye
but last year alone America dropped
26,171* bombs on brown bodies,
on our trees and animals and homes.
That's 235,539 months or 19,628 years
to process the devastation of one.
Honestly, I am unsure of the maths.
Give or take a week, millenniums
are still owed to the lost. I don't know
how to calculate for the land or
the numbers for the unlucky survivors,
the dust-strewn rubble-reapers looking
for family in red rocks, for burned
paper that might hold a shred of name,
for safe waters that will not drown
them, for borders that will not cut
their feet or demand they unstitch
history from their backs. Call it
an ugly flag. Plant a new one
in their mouths. This kind of loss
has not been measured, it has no body
count, but we have all the time
in the world to weigh it now.
We have all the time in the world.

*When I wrote this poem in 2017, I
was referring to statistics from 2016.
As I write this in 2018, I can tell you
that in 2017 America dropped 40,000
bombs. From 2014 to 2017, a total of
94,000 bombs. In my lifetime alone,
the sheer tonnage of destruction and
chaos that has been unleashed on
majority Muslim or Arab nations has
been nothing short of catastrophic, year
after year of staggering violence which
the population of Western countries
seem to accept. Go back further, past
my lifetime, my mother's, and into
my grandfather's and you will still
find ample military campaigns and
Western-backed violences to highlight
the sustained injustice against Arab
peoples. You could not do this to those
you saw as fully human. Though I had
not the heart to seek out the full body
count of Iraqis, Afghanis, Syrians,
Yemenis, Palestinians — the refugees
drowned in wave after generational
wave of forced migration, of certain
death at home or a bleakening hope
abroad — the munitions alone tell a
deadly, horrifying story.

IN — THE — NINETY-THIRD — YEAR — OF — SETTLEMENT — THE — COLONY — SUFFERED — A — CATACLYSMIC — COLLAPSE / FAR — IN — THE — OUTER — REACHES — OF — THE — CONSTELLATION — OF — THE — EAGLE / TWIN-STAR — SYSTEM / WHERE — RED — AND — BLUE — SUNS — CIRCLE — EACH — IN — EVERLASTING — NIGHT / IN — EVERLASTING — NIGHT / TREMORS — SHOOK / AN — EXPLODING — STAR — RAINED — FIRE — UPON — THE — HOST / WE — LOST — CONTACT / UPON — THE — SURFACE — A — GREAT — CLOUD — GREW / AND — BENEATH — IT — LAY — THE — DOOMED — CITIES — OF — THE — PLAIN / OBSCURED / THE — RED — DAWN — BROKE / WHAT — SERE — DAY — AWAITS — OUR — HEROES — ON — THE — OTHER — SIDE / THOSE — CHILDREN — OF — THE — NEXT — AND — LAST — FRONTIER — WHO — SLEEP / PERHAPS DREAM / OUR — HOPES — UPON — THE — SCORCHED — SURFACE — OBLITERATED / IN — THE — SLOW — PATH — OF — THE — OBLITERATING — MACHINE / WE — HAVE — NOT — WAKED / NOR — SLEPT — OUR — FITFUL — FLIGHT — THE — DUST — AND — FIRE / THROUGH — CENTURIES — PRESENT — CALAMITY / WE — LOST — CONTACT / AT — AN — ALTITUDE — OF — TWO — THOUSAND — THOUSAND / HURTLING — TOWARD — UNKNOWN — LIGHT / FATAL — HEART — OF — THE — EXPLODING — STAR / ALL — OUR — HOPES / ALL — DUST / WE — SEND — TO — YOU / SISTER — EARTH / TRANSMISSION — FROM — A — SMALL — AND — DISTANT — WORLD / TO — SURVIVE — YOUR — TIME — AND — WAKE / SO — YOU — MAY — LIVE / INTO — OURS

Note: Voyager's Golden Record, launched into space in 1977, carried the following message from Earth: 'This is a present from a small, distant world ... We are attempting to survive our time so we may live into yours'.

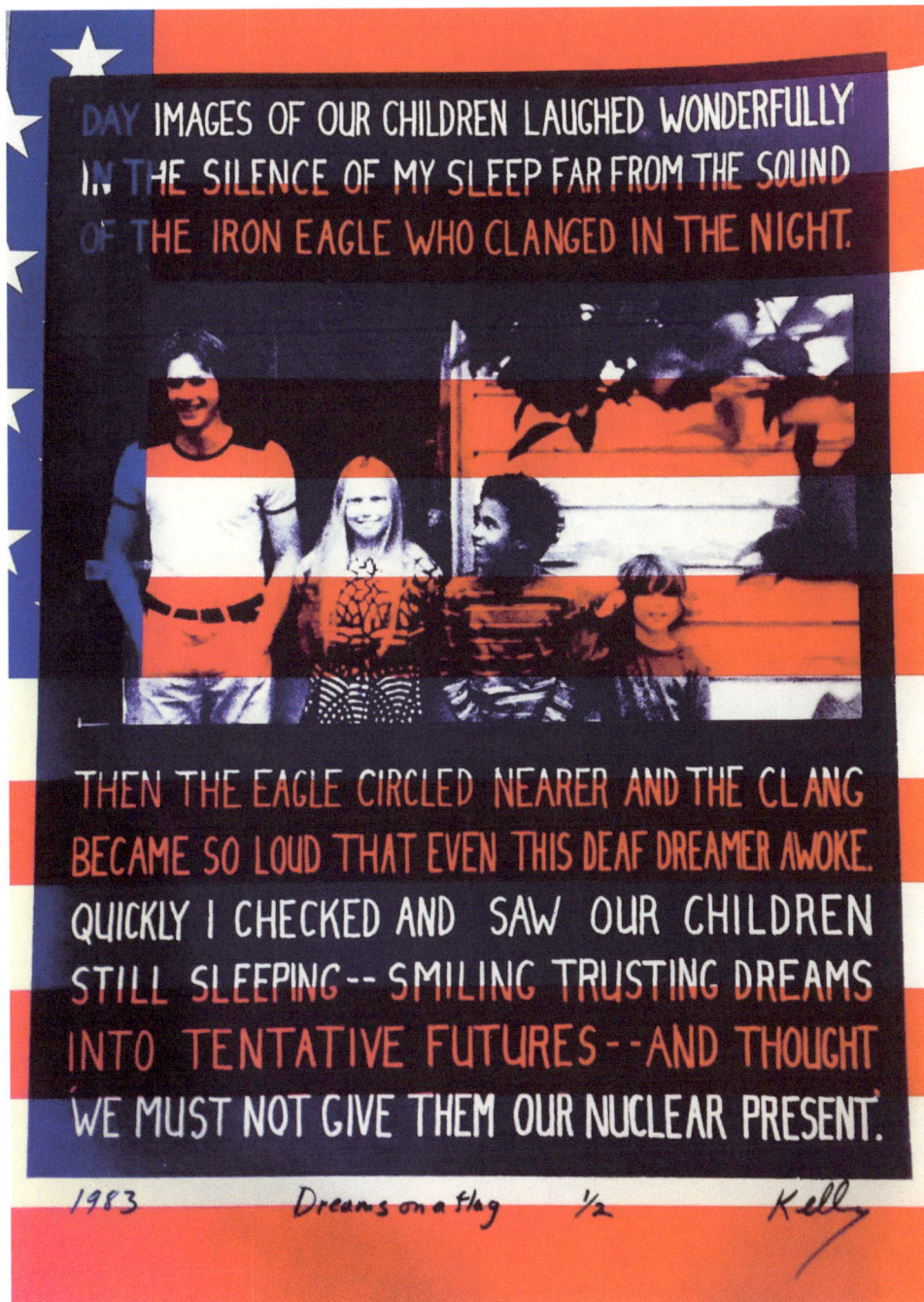

DAY IMAGES OF OUR CHILDREN LAUGHED WONDERFULLY IN THE SILENCE OF MY SLEEP FAR FROM THE SOUND OF THE IRON EAGLE WHO CLANGED IN THE NIGHT.

THEN THE EAGLE CIRCLED NEARER AND THE CLANG BECAME SO LOUD THAT EVEN THIS DEAF DREAMER AWOKE. QUICKLY I CHECKED AND SAW OUR CHILDREN STILL SLEEPING -- SMILING TRUSTING DREAMS INTO TENTATIVE FUTURES -- AND THOUGHT WE MUST NOT GIVE THEM OUR NUCLEAR PRESENT.

1983   Dreams on a flag   ½   Kelly

William Kelly **Dreams on a Flag**

1983, silkscreen on offset lithograph flag image, c. 56 x 38 cm.

William Kelly **Tender Dreams / Tentative Futures II**

2010, digital print on archival paper, 29.5 x 21 cm.

Ours is a time of rapid transition, but to an uncertain destination — a time of turbulence when the old is dying, but the new has yet to be born. Two world wars, the Great Depression, the Holocaust, the advent of nuclear weapons, the Cold War and more recently climate change, itself emblematic of a more pervasive ecological crisis, a series of pandemics, financial crises, drone warfare and terrorist attacks leave little doubt that we are going through a profound social and ecological upheaval.

Violence has become endemic. The number of armed conflicts in the world has risen steadily since 1946 and now stands at 50 or more in any one year. Equally revealing is the trendline in forcible displacements. By the end of 2019, 79.5 million persons were forcibly displaced worldwide as a result of persecution, conflict, violence, or human rights violations. As of mid-January 2021, the COVID-19 pandemic had reached nearly 93 million cases and 2 million deaths.

In the most thorough planetary health check ever undertaken, the 2019 UN Global Assessment Report tells us that nature is being destroyed at a rate tens to hundreds of times higher than the average over the past 10 million years. The biomass of wild mammals has fallen by 82%, natural ecosystems have lost about half their area and a million species are at risk of extinction — all this largely the result of human actions

It is becoming clearer by the day that these are not isolated disturbances, but the symptoms of a deeper ailment, which should be diagnosed and treated holistically. An integrated approach to the multiple challenges that now threaten humanity and the entire Earth community is the ethical and practical imperative of our time.

Such an approach views justice, peace and respect for nature as inextricably linked. The many unresolved conflicts around the world desperately call for peacemaking and peacebuilding initiatives but these will not go far unless they are sensitive to the cries of the poor and the cries of the Earth. Simply put, we have no option but to strive for a just and ecologically sustainable peace.

How relevant, you may ask, is all this to Australia's present circumstances? If what is proposed is a holistic approach to the problem of violence that encompasses social and ecological violence as well as physical violence, is Australia capable of adopting this approach in its societal arrangements and relations with the rest of the world? To judge by the parlous state of Australian politics and public discourse, at least as filtered by mainstream media, the omens are less than propitious. And yet, the possibilities are immense and tantalising, and the ground potentially more fertile than is often supposed.

A case in point is the failure of successive Australian governments to devise an energy policy that delivers a low carbon economy and affordable energy for those on low incomes. As of now Australia is struggling to meet the modest 2030 target set by the Paris agreement of 26–28% reduction in national emissions compared to 2005 levels. This is a laughably low target when compared to that set for other advanced economies, and much lower than what is both desirable and feasible — many experts have argued persuasively for a target of zero emissions by 2050.

The energy policy vacuum has proved especially damaging for our relations with Pacific neighbours. Rather than empathise with the concerns of Pacific Island nations for whom climate change is an existential threat, the Australian government has turned a deaf ear to their pleas and focused instead on containing Chinese influence in the region. The former prime minister of Tuvalu revealed that he was 'stunned' by Scott Morrison's attitude at the 2019 Pacific Islands Forum, in particular by the suggestion that Pacific leaders should 'take the money ... then shut up about climate change'.

Yet, Pacific leaders have stated repeatedly that time is running out for their countries. If global emissions are not drastically reduced, thousands of low-lying atolls may become uninhabitable within decades, and other threats could come a whole lot sooner. As sea levels rise, the likelihood is that some islands will run out of freshwater long before they run out of land. On most Pacific islands, freshwater is already an imperilled resource.

The exodus of environmental refugees, not just from the Pacific but from the coastal regions of South Asia and parts of Southeast Asia, is expected to become a major security threat over the next ten to twenty years. With climate change and other environmental pressures already reducing the availability of water, food and arable land in host countries, transboundary migration is expected to rise sharply, exacerbating tensions and conflict within and between countries.

How should Australia respond? Until now Australian governments have viewed these trends largely through a military lens, which explains the 'children overboard' fiasco in 2001, the military-led 'operation sovereign borders' established in 2013, and the continuing policy of offshore detention. This has meant preventing seriously sick detainees from coming to Australia for urgent medical treatment, or endlessly delaying treatment once they have made it to the mainland. Underlying it all is a conscious policy to make victims of humanitarian crises the primary targets of our insecurity.

A just peace approach to such complex challenges as climate change, refugee flows, humanitarian crises would be radically different in both content and process. So would the way we handle gross human rights violations in our neighbourhood, and military tensions and conflicts, whether in Afghanistan, the South China Sea, Korea or further afield.

The very first step for the nation must be to reach agreement on a statement of principles arrived at after extensive community consultation. Such a statement would begin by acknowledging the colonisation and dispossession of Indigenous people in Australia and the urgent need to establish a new social contract that restores equality and dignity to the relationship. At the same time, Australia is facing a seismic shift that is simultaneously geopolitical, cultural and ecological. The shift in the centre of economic gravity and political influence from the West to the East makes it all the more imperative for Australia to reconcile its history and geography.

The proposed statement of principles would place the emphasis not on military alliances or militarised notions of security but on human and ecological security. The overriding commitment would be to protect persons, communities and nature and respect the diverse histories, cultures, and faiths that make up Australia.

This political and cultural reorientation would make possible a number of long overdue initiatives. The first would be to set in train a process of steady disengagement from ANZUS, a nuclear and conventional alliance with the United States, which has consistently led to military engagements that exacerbate conflicts, deepen sectarian hatreds, and further destabilise already vulnerable societies. A non-aligned Australia would be much better placed to support nuclear disarmament, and actively work with others to bring to fruition the Treaty on the Prohibition of Nuclear Weapons.

The second closely related step would be to apply the principle of international good citizenship to a large and complex set of relationships that have been dangerously neglected. A high priority should be to reengage and actively collaborate with all arms of the UN system, and in concert with like-minded members seek to renew and reform the institution. Equally there is a crying need to recalibrate our relations with Asian neighbours with a view to developing a regional framework actively pursuing preventive diplomacy, the peaceful settlement of disputes and humane management of refugee flows. All of which depends in part on concerted action to repair the damage that high levels of economic growth over the last three decades have inflicted on the natural environment, not just climate change but loss of biodiversity, degraded forests, alpine, wetland, and coastal ecosystems and increased waste and pollution from rapidly expanding and poorly planned urbanisation.

In pursuing this course, Australia cannot focus exclusively on its own security, especially if this means acting in ways other nations perceive to be at the expense of their security. With almost every actual or potential conflict of concern to Australia, the key to its resolution lies in reconciling the competing security interests of different actors. This applies equally to China's rise, Sino-Japanese tensions, rivalries in the South China Sea, the Korean conflict, climate change and refugee flows. In other words, 'common security' for all stakeholders is the only viable security policy.

Of course, coming to terms with the requirements of common security is no easy task. No single authority or government can impose on others what the concept means or how it is to be applied. It follows that if we are to develop an effective suite of policies based on the principles of a just and ecologically sustainable peace, civil society in Australia must be fully engaged. This should include not only think-tanks congenial to government thinking, business interests or influential lobby groups but also religious, humanitarian, professional, educational and other institutions with relevant insights, expertise, resources and contacts. Beyond this, media must play their part, for without the consistent airing of accurate information, analysis and ideas, policies are likely to falter in the longer term.

The crucial role of civil society cannot be overstated. The kind of policies and decision-making processes we adopt ultimately depend on Australia's social fabric. If just peace principles are to apply, then society needs to rethink what it understands by the 'terrorist' threat, how it has come about, and what sustains groups and individuals attracted to violent extremism. It requires society to question xenophobic attitudes and in particular the Islamophobia and China bashing that now colour so much of our security policies at home and abroad. We need a mature national conversation on our national security and terrorism laws and the vastly expanded powers and budgets we have invested in our security establishment, and the implications of all this for civil liberties, democratic institutions, social cohesion, religious and cultural dialogue and much else.

As we have seen, the same can be said of policies relating to energy security and climate change, 'border protection' and the treatment of refugees and asylum seekers. What is in question is not just how a particular problem or threat is dealt with, but how any given response will impact on the ethical and institutional foundations of society. Whether one considers the laws of armed conflict, the nuclear ban treaty, or the growing body of international human rights and environmental law, it is not simply a question of Australia signing up to this or that legal instrument, important as this is, but ensuring that the new legal norms are embedded in the mindset, mores and discourse of society as a whole.

A just and ecologically sustainable peace is an emerging paradigm that can help Australia construct a narrative that reinterprets our past and reimagines our future. Such a narrative could begin to heal the wounds of Indigenous dispossession and colonial violence. Importantly, it could overcome the destructive separation of nature and culture and, informed by Indigenous wisdom, learn to solve human problems by greater attentiveness to the needs and rhythms of other species and the wider ecological processes in which we participate. Lastly, it could provide a more coherent policy framework that integrates economic needs, environmental values, educational aspirations, and the rich possibilities offered by the dialogue of cultures, religions and civilisations.

Further Reading

— Amster, Randall. *Peace Ecology*. Boulder, CO: Paradigm Publishers, 2015.

—Camilleri, Joseph. 'It's Time to Strip "national security" of its Sacred Cow Status'. A 3-part article in *Pearls and Irritations*, 6-8 July 2020, https://johnmenadue.com/joseph-camilleri-its-time-to-strip-national-security-of-its-sacred-cow-status-part-1/ (accessed 3 March 2021).

—Hope, Sr., Kempe Ronald. 'Peace, Justice and Inclusive Institutions: Overcoming Challenges to the Implementation of Sustainable Development Goal 16'. *Global Change, Peace & Security* 32, no. 1 (2020): 57–77, https://www.tandfonline.com/doi/abs/10.1080/14781158.2019.1667320?journalCode=cpar20(accessed 3 March 2021).

— Starting, Rebecca, and Jasmine-Kim Westendorf. 'Introduction: A Critical Analysis of Australian Foreign, Defence and Strategic Policy', *Australian Journal of International Affairs* 74, no. 3 (2020): 208–12.

— UNDRR (United Nations Office for Disaster Risk Reduction). *Global Assessment Report on Disaster Risk Reduction* (GAR 2019), https://gar.undrr.org/ (accessed 12 January 2021).

— Virji, Hassan, Ayyoob Sharifi, Shinji Kaneko, and Dahlia Simangan. 'The Sustainability–Peace Nexus in the Context of Global Change', *Sustainable Science* 14 (2019): 1467–68, https://doi.org/10.1007/s11625-019-00737-1 (accessed 3 March 2021).

Recent surveys show that experiences of profound communion with the aliveness of the Universe are not a fringe phenomenon but, instead, are familiar encounters for a large portion of the public. ... When we see ourselves as participants in a cosmic garden of life that has been developing patiently over billions of years, our regard for the universe shifts from indifference, fear, and cynicism to curiosity, love, and awe. Humanity's future pivots on which understanding prevails and the choices that naturally follow.[1]

Amazing scientific discoveries at a super-macro and super-micro level are completely changing our understanding of the human's place in creation. Cosmic consciousness is affecting who we are, how we live, everything we do — the ground has shifted; the context for every dimension of life is different. Many of those who were dominating and extracting are learning to live with and respect the whole earth community and the cosmos. That sounds a lot more positive than the facts might warrant, but the seeds of deep transformation are planted and — if we humans are going to survive on this planet — they have to be carefully tended.

At the same time, also beginning to come into focus is an astoundingly widespread interest in nonviolence as an orientation and a universal ethic that decidedly stands against all forms of violence — from the violence being inflicted on the Amazon to the immense violence facing migrants; from the cataclysmic violence of war to the violence of economic inequality; from the violence of nuclear weapons to the violence of human trafficking and racism. Nonviolence is a spirituality and a way of life. It is also a set of powerful practices for negotiating conflict, untying the knots of systemic injustice and promoting right relationships among people and with the whole earth community.

In *Laudato Si'* and elsewhere, Pope Francis speaks about integral ecology, integral human development, integral peace. The issues, the challenges we face are intertwined, interconnected at a root deep level and have been made even more visible by the coronavirus pandemic. For example, persistent poverty and the huge gap between the very rich and the many impoverished are connected as cause and consequence to war and violent conflict, and both are connected (again, as cause and consequence) to environmental destruction and climate change. No matter what is your point of entry, you will arrive at a knot of systemic injustice that has many expressions but similar roots and potentially catastrophic consequences for human life and ecological integrity.

In Peru, a local organisation, Human Rights and Environment, Puno (DHUMA), works closely with Indigenous communities who are making their voices heard through strategic litigation to resist destructive extractive projects, but also to establish precedents and jurisprudence that will strengthen the legal framework for preventing and resolving conflicts in the future. DHUMA is dedicated to teaching, defending, and making it possible to enforce the rights of Indigenous peoples and the rights of Mother Earth, especially in the area of water, endangered by climate change and severe contamination caused by mining. In 2011 more than 20,000 peasant farmers from Aymara communities mobilised to defend their territory and their right to water. They gave a firm 'No' to the presence of a major mining project owned by a Canadian company.

Pax Christi International is a global Catholic peace movement with 120 member organisations working for peace on six continents. For 75 years, Pax Christi International members around the world, including many who have lived in extremely dangerous situations, have nurtured a deep commitment to active nonviolence. About ten years ago we began to collect stories about the methodology and impact, success or failure, faith-connection or not of nonviolent practice from different, often very violent contexts where our members live or work. We began to see amazing creativity, wisdom and, frequently, the effectiveness of nonviolent strategies despite the fact that nonviolent options were often dismissed as passive, even irresponsible in the 'real' world and were almost always under-resourced.

We were tired of being dismissed as naive when we challenged violent responses to threatened or actual violence, especially when one of the great gifts of our age is the empirical evidence that active nonviolence is a positive, constructive and powerful force for social change. A diverse set of nonviolent approaches — from diplomacy to trauma healing, from restorative justice to accompaniment, from civil resistance to music and humour — are effectively dealing with violence without lethal force; transforming conflict; protecting people, communities and the Earth at risk; fostering just and peaceful alternatives.

As a Catholic movement we began to realise that it could make a huge difference in knowledge about and the development of nonviolent approaches to conflict transformation if the Catholic Church turned its vast capacity for education, communication, advocacy and diplomacy to teaching about nonviolence, researching the effectiveness of different nonviolent options, advocating for public policies that support and promote nonviolent approaches to national and international security.

What if 1.3 billion Catholics worldwide were formed from the beginning of life to understand and appreciate the power and effectiveness of active nonviolence and the connection of nonviolence to the heart of the Gospel? What if we all knew how to apply nonviolent tools to defuse conflict before it became violent?

What if the Catholic Church committed its vast spiritual, intellectual and financial resources to developing a new moral framework and language for discerning ways to prevent atrocities, to protect people and the planet in a dangerous world? What would happen if the Church left behind easy references to 'just war' and prioritised nonviolent tools to address violent or potentially violent situations?

45

For the past five years, the Catholic Nonviolence Initiative, a project of Pax Christi International, has been working to bring nonviolence from the periphery of Catholic thought and teaching to the centre — to mainstream nonviolence as a spirituality, a style of life, a program for societal action, and a universal ethic. The energetic, positive international response to this effort from both inside and outside the Church has been remarkable. The Initiative doesn't pretend to have the last word about active nonviolence; rather, it specifically encourages people to learn from local experience how to live nonviolently in their own context, how to employ nonviolence wherever they are in the service of just peace and ecological integrity.

We now know about the consequences of violence — physical, economic, psychological and ecological — and we have witnessed over and over violence failing to accomplish whatever was its stated purpose, and violence begetting more violence. It is evident that if we are ever to achieve the kind of just peace and ecological integrity for which we all long, the global community needs to give vastly more intellectual and financial resources, creativity and courage to developing effective conflict prevention, peace building and other nonviolent tools.

---

1. Duane Elgin, 'We Are Bio-Cosmic Beings Learning to Live in a Living Universe', *Kosmos* (Fall/Winter 2017), https://www.kosmosjournal.org/article/we-are-bio-cosmic-beings-learning-to-live-in-a-living-universe/ (accessed 12 January 2021).

Further Reading
— Berger, Rose Marie, Ken Butigan, Judy Coode, and Marie Dennis, eds. *Advancing Nonviolence and Just Peace in the Church and the World.* Brussels: Pax Christi International, 2020.
— Campaign Nonviolence: A Project of Pace e Bene Nonviolence Service, https://paceebene.org/ (accessed 12 January 2021).
— Catholic Nonviolence Initiative, https://nonviolencejustpeace.net/ (accessed 12 January 2021).
— Dennis, Marie, ed. *Choosing Peace: The Catholic Church Returns to Gospel Nonviolence.* New York: Orbis Books, 2018.
— Pax Christi International, https://paxchristi.net/ (accessed 12 January 2021).
— Pelicaric, Veronica, and Nina Koevoets. *Engaging Nonviolence: Activating Nonviolent Change in Our Lives and Our World.* Corvallis, OR: Pace e Bene Press, 2019.
— Pope Francis. *Laudato Si': On Care for Our Common Home: An Encyclical Letter on Ecology and Climate* (24 May 2015). Strathfield, NSW: St Paul Publications, 2015. Available online: http://www.vatican.va/content/francesco/en/encyclicals/documents/papa-francesco_20150524_enciclica-laudato-si.html (accessed 12 January 2021).
— Pope Francis. 'Nonviolence: A Style of Politics for Peace'. Message of His Holiness Pope Francis for the Celebration of the Fiftieth World Day of Peace, 1 January 2017, https://w2.vatican.va/content/francesco/en/messages/peace/documents/papa-francesco_20161208_messaggio-l-giornata-mondiale-pace-2017.html (accessed 12 January 2021).

The biblical traditions share the teaching that humanity is made 'in the image of God',[1] by which we mean not that we all look physically like God, of course, but that we each have a soul, a divine spark or an element of God in us — and it immediately follows that we each have rights to be free, to have a share in the common wealth of humanity, which includes food, water, energy, education, health, meaningful employment, etc. It also means that it should not matter whether a person is male, female or however they define themselves — or gay or straight, asexual or somewhere on the continuum. It should be immaterial what colour, race or religion they are (or are not) — God loves each of us equally, and we need to have a society that encourages love, respect, care and concern, support, and a genuine interest in who people are, where they have come from and to what they aspire.

It is quite easy to be welcoming of people like ourselves. And our traditions teach us repeatedly to 'love our neighbour' as well as to welcome the stranger,[2] for we were strangers in the land of Egypt. But at some point, we come to our limits (as we have found in Australia and around the world). Do we welcome those very different or who we may have reason to be scared of? Refugees — of different colour and faith? How do we integrate and support those, some of whom may have been murderers, or who harbour hatred or speak vitriol or plot terrorism? We tend to want to demonstrate the benefits, the 'superiority', of living like we do, to persuade newcomers to change, to be not 'in the image of God', but in our own image. We have a lot of work to do to recognise that others may have experiences and viewpoints very different from ours — and reason to hold on to them. As we say in one of our prayers, we should learn to give thanks 'for human community, our common past and future hope, our oneness transcending all separation, our capacity to work for peace and justice even in the midst of hostility and oppression'.[3]

As I listed earlier, at the top of the physical rights for every human being are food, water and energy. If we don't ensure these in fair and reasonable degree, then there is no chance of a just peace — only an enforced and temporary illusion (amongst the ignorant or unaware beneficiaries) of peace, when the 'others' are subjugated, hungry and thirsty, and we know that that is not only unjust, but will inevitably have great costs, and a limited duration before fomenting revolution, and usually a bloody one.

Many of us tend to take a visit to the market or supermarket for granted. Never before has there been such a wide and rich selection of foods available. But we need to remember that we are a minority — in many parts of the world, this would be their idea of heaven, and even in Australia, there are many who see it, but cannot afford it, and resort to cheaper (and frequently the less healthy) alternatives. Famines are not new to the world — many go hungry, and indeed, even today, many die from famine and malnutrition-related causes. In the Torah, famine was a common occurrence. But we read in particular about Egypt, where Joseph is said to have predicted seven years of plenty, followed by seven years of famine. His solution was to build store cities and collect the surplus — the original 'grain mountain'.[4] This was then shared out during the famine — and there was apparently even enough for visitors from neighbouring countries — but it cost them, both visitors and locals alike! By the end of the famine, the people were impoverished and indentured. We need to acknowledge that there will be costs. We don't need to eat (and waste) as much as we do — and we should not be expecting food to be flown round the world for us, causing huge additional impacts in the process. Food is likely to become somewhat more expensive.

Whilst we are already seeing drought and flood severely affecting food production, some predictions show dramatic reductions as temperatures rise. Whilst arable land available will shrink, populations continue to grow. The world's population, currently just under 8 billion, many of whom already do not have enough to eat, will reach over 11 billion by 2100.[5] Even if production levels stay as they are, what will those 3 billion extra eat? We are likely facing massive unfolding starvation but we continue to reassure ourselves that 'we'll be OK' — at the expense of other human beings and animals just as much created in God's image and deserving of life as we are.

Water too is of course crucial. Rapidly-receding glaciers will have a direct impact on ten of the world's major river systems which originate in the Himalayas, increasing the risk of flooding in summers and eventually causing drought as the ice disappears. This would affect 1.9 billion people who live downstream as well as 3 billion people who rely on crops grown in the river basins.[6] And in many places they can't get water at all, as drought follows drought, as we know even from rural Australia where many towns are even now reliant on water tankers.[7]

Water has long been a potent issue in the Middle East. Isaac in Genesis upsets the local shepherds when he draws water, repeatedly moving to old or new wells until finally he can live in peace.[8] Today he would not be so lucky. Experts reckon that the region stopped having enough water for its needs in the 1970s. And the situation has deteriorated since then, thanks to population growth and climate change. But the predicted conflicts over water resources have not yet materialised. Water security was a key part of the peace agreement between Israel and Jordan which has now endured since 1994. It contains a water sharing agreement, determining that Jordan should receive 50 million cubic meters per year from Israel. Israel has managed this by building huge reservoirs and massive desalination plants, and by developing advanced recycling — Israel recycles 87 percent of its wastewater, compared to 20 percent by Spain, its nearest rival.[9] It also made huge savings in agricultural water use by developing drip irrigation, now used throughout the world.

Energy is required for the most basic needs, like pumping water to have domestic taps rather than distant wells. For light to read and study. For power for heat and cooling fans, and phones and computers to operate businesses.

And fuel to power vehicles to get to shops and hospitals and to collect goods and make deliveries.

Just as mobile phones enabled poor villages to skip land lines, solar can help them avoid the local and international dangers of fossil fuels. More resilience, less infrastructure, less cost — and far less damage to the environment. It is a no brainer, and we and our leaders must stand up against the dinosaurs of the fossil fuel industries and transition to clean energy, bringing with it more and safer and better employment, and the hope of a better, safer, more just and more peaceful world to pass on to those who come after us.

1. Genesis 1:26 (*b'tzelem elohim*).

2. 36 times in Torah — the 'Five Books of Moses', e.g., Leviticus 19:34.

3. *Mishkan T'filah* World Union Edition Shabbat and Daily Prayer Book, CCAR 2010, *Modim*, 257.

4. Genesis 41:35.

5. 'Middle Projection', Projected World Population, Business Insider, http://static1.businessinsider.com/image/55b937bc2acae74c2f8b8d20-1200-900/world-population-projection.png (accessed 12 January 2021).

6. Deutsche Welle, 'Living in Hope and Fear Beside India's Himalayan Glaciers', EcoWatch, https://www.ecowatch.com/india-himalayan-glaciers-water-2641354174.html?rebelltitem=8#rebelltitem8 (accessed 12 January 2021).

7. Shannon Molloy, 'The Towns Forced to Pay $1 Million a Month to Stay Alive as Drought Crisis Worsens', News Corp Australia network, https://www.news.com.au/national/the-towns-forced-to-pay-1-million-a-month-just-to-stay-alive-as-drought-crisis-worsens/news-story/5feed90428a4007cc10d3894880ac65c (accessed 12 January 2021).

8. Genesis 26:22.

9. Zafrir Rinat, 'Israel Is Undisputed World Leader in Using Purified Wastewater for Crops', *Haaretz*, https://www.haaretz.com/life/.premium-israel-is-undisputed-champion-in-using-purified-wastewater-for-crops-1.5472512 (accessed 12 January 2021).

William Kelly **Childhoods**

2018, lithograph, 19 x 15 cm.

After 'Childhoods' by William Kelly

(i)
At the centre of things,
mouth fastens to breast,
an infant claims his mother's hair
as a supplicant clings to a hem.

If he falls
If he falls—
some worlds are rimmed in wire.

(ii)
When wire thatches shadow,
a woman stands alone
clutching her heart or her belly;
between mother and child,
a huddle unnamed as stones—

(iii)
Here, Aylan is held.
Picasso's limp child is held.
The ladder is not broken.
Ascension is dubious.

(iv)
The girl and her hoop are cut from the street.
Beyond melancholy, she runs
as if to outpace her shadow—
Alice is chasing her own rabbit hole,
she may not fall,
but she must keep running.

And the glass-eyed girl,
too young to run,
her smile, fixed as a postage stamp,
gazes at the world.

———

As a first-year medical student at Flinders University in Adelaide, I found myself at a global congress in Beijing, China. My introduction to the doctors' peace movement had come some months earlier when I answered an email from Professor Ian Maddocks of the Medical Association for the Prevention of War (MAPW) asking if any medical students would like to apply for funding to attend the biennial gathering of the International Physicians for the Prevention of Nuclear War (IPPNW). As someone who had been drawn to medicine not only for the opportunity to mediate healing, but also by the possibility of an increased platform for advocacy, I leapt at this opportunity. Surrounded by medical students and doctors from all over the world, I attended a student-led session one morning at which we were asked to work together in groups, brainstorming a better future and writing our thoughts on large sheets of butcher paper. I will never forget the moment when Dr Ira Helfand, at the time the head of a large department of emergency medicine in the United States, a senior and experienced anti-nuclear campaigner, sat down on the floor next to me, and humbly participated in this activity. This was in stark contrast to the hierarchical world of medicine I was entering in my studies.

To sit down and listen is at the very core of both good clinical medicine and transformational peace activism. The discipline of becoming a trained observer and an active listener is a lifelong pursuit. The peace and social justice traditions in the medical profession run deep. In the work to abolish nuclear weapons, the stories of nuclear survivors, including those of the Hibakusha, survivors of the nuclear bombings of Hiroshima and Nagasaki in Japan, the Aboriginal people of Australia, our Pacific Island neighbours, and indeed, survivor communities from around the world, ground and inform a global movement. We weave together the scientific understanding of the impact of nuclear weapons on human health and the environment with the stories and narratives of destruction and devastation from the traditional owners of the land we live on.

My own journey as a doctor and an activist mirrors the development of the International Campaign for the Abolition of Nuclear Weapons (ICAN). It was in my second year of medical school when the visionary Malaysian obstetrician Dr Ron McCoy had the idea that a global campaign with a singular focus was what was needed to overcome the inertia and cynicism occurring at the international level, with little to no progress in the work of the Non-Proliferation Treaty (NPT). A small group of enthusiastic Australians took up that challenge, and in 2006 ICAN was born in Melbourne. Building on decades of diligent hard work and courageous activism, the campaign sought to build a groundswell of public opposition to the worst weapons of mass destruction ever created. As I finished medical school the next year, the campaign which had been birthed from within the Medical Association for the Prevention of War (MAPW) and endorsed by the International Physicians for the Prevention of Nuclear War (IPPNW) was launched in Melbourne and then Vienna.

As ICAN has grown, the vision has coalesced into the Treaty on the Prohibition of Nuclear Weapons (TPNW), which addresses a legal gap in international law. Until now there have been treaties banning biological and chemical weapons, land mines and cluster bombs, but no overarching treaty making the possession, use or threat of use of nuclear weapons illegal. Over 50 countries have now ratified the treaty, and it entered into force on 22 January 2021.

As I have grown as a doctor, and become a neurosurgeon, the discipline of listening to my patients has been deeply instilled in me. Often, by carefully taking a history a diagnosis can be reached, and life-changing treatment can begin. Other times the patient in front of me has a condition which overwhelms the ability of modern medicine to treat and cure. And it is those patients who have taught me the power of bearing witness. Listening to the pain and hearing the stories of suffering, acknowledging the journey and sitting in solidarity are my only offerings for these patients. And yet even in these moments, there creeps in a hope, that someday, we might be able to do more, and better, for these patients. And as I have learned to listen to my patients, I believe the global movement for nuclear abolition has been learning to listen to the Hibakusha. On December 10, 2017, ICAN received the Nobel Peace Prize for our 'work to draw attention to the catastrophic humanitarian consequences of any use of nuclear weapons and for its ground-breaking efforts to achieve a treaty-based prohibition on such weapons'.[1] On that day Setsuko Thurlow, who was only 13 when she survived the atomic bombing of Hiroshima, accepted the Prize on our behalf, along with Beatrice Fihn, our Executive Director. Never before has a Hibakusha been at the podium to receive a Nobel Peace Prize, even though the Prize has been awarded 12 times for anti-nuclear work.

On the eve of the 50th ratification of the TPNW, Setsuko shared her reflections on learning the treaty was reaching this critical step:

> As I sat in my chair, I found myself speaking with the spirits of hundreds of thousands of people who lost their lives in Hiroshima and Nagasaki. I was immediately in conversation with these beloved souls — my sister, my nephew Eiji, other dear family members, my classmates, all the children and innocent people who perished. I was reporting to the dead, sharing this good news first with them, because they paid the ultimate price with their precious lives. Like many survivors, I made a vow that their deaths would not be in vain and to warn the world about the danger of nuclear weapons, to make sure that no one else suffers as we have suffered. I made a vow to work for nuclear disarmament until my last breath. And now we have reached a milestone in our decades' long struggle — the Treaty on the Prohibition of Nuclear Weapons will become international law![2]

As the good news of this treaty spreads, and the global groundswell of public opposition becomes international law, I take great courage from the image of Setsuko, reporting to the dead, the cloud of witnesses.

It remains our task to report to the living, those who have not yet heard, that there are still 13,000 nuclear weapons in existence which threaten not only human existence but the planet on which we live. As ICAN has its origins amongst doctors and medical students and other activists, so our work for the abolition of nuclear weapons draws strength and depth from the stories from the bedside — the burns, the cancers, the birth defects, the deaths. Towards a just and ecologically sustainable peace, we work, together.

1. 'The Nobel Peace Prize for 2017', The Nobel Prize, https://www.nobelprize.org/prizes/peace/2017/press-release/ (accessed 12 January 2021).
2. Setsuko Thurlow, 'The TPNW — A Game Changer in Nuclear Disarmament', ICAN, https://www.icanw.org/setsuko_thurlow_statement_on_tpnw_entry_into_force (accessed 12 January 2021).

Further Reading
— ICAN. 'Choosing Humanity: Why Australia Must Join the Treaty on the Prohibition of Nuclear Weapons' (July 2019), https://icanw.org.au/wp-content/uploads/Choosing-Humanity-ICAN-Report.pdf (accessed 3 March 2021).
— ICAN. 'For the Record … Addressing the Australian Government's Misrepresentation of the UN Treaty on the Prohibition of Nuclear Weapons' (November 2020), https://icanw.org.au/wp-content uploads/For-the-record_Nov-2020_web.pdf (accessed 3 March 2021).
— United Nations General Assembly. *Treaty on the Prohibition of Nuclear Weapons*, https://documents-dds-ny.un.org/doc/UNDOC/GEN/N17/209/73/PDF/N1720973.pdf?OpenElement (accessed 3 March 2021).

If you see in a province the oppression of the poor and the violation
of justice and right, do not be amazed at the matter; for the high official
is watched by a higher, and there are yet higher ones over them.
(Ecclesiastes 5:8 NRSV)

Australia is weary of Afghanistan, our longest war on foreign soil. Australia's
overt military involvement began in October 2001, part of a multifaceted
international intervention. Although Australia's contribution officially ended
in 2013, Australian Defence Force (ADF) personnel continued to be deployed
in a range of roles into 2021.[1] In October 2013, then Prime Minister Tony
Abbott addressed a gathering at the Australian base in Uruzgan: 'Australia's
longest war is ending. Not with victory, not with defeat, but with, we hope, an
Afghanistan that is better for our presence here'.[2]

Is Afghanistan better for Australia's military presence? The answer is
not certain. It depends on whom you ask. Sharp differences of perspective
reflect deepening demographic and cultural divides within Afghanistan.
We Australians most often encounter formally educated urban or diaspora
Afghans, yet half the population are illiterate and three quarters live in rural
areas.[3] Less than four percent of Afghans use the internet, yet some live on
social media. The answer also depends on the willingness to risk a straight
answer. As Afghans say, 'Look at the sky, and choose your turban'. In other
words, do and say whatever reassures whichever planes, drones or satellites,
soldiers or spies, are watching.

I was fortunate to first live and work in Afghanistan before Australia was
an occupying force when Afghans still welcomed us as guests. I spent most of
those early years in rural villages. That shaped my perspective. During later
seasons, I moved through urban and rural regions working with humanitarian
organisations that were intentionally impartial in the conflict. That shaped
my perspective too. As an outsider, I do not speak for Afghanistan or any of its
people. Yet, I hope that sharing these fragments of remembered conversations
might help other Australians cultivate a more empathetic and intuitive sense
of the experiences, courage, hopes and fears, of some Afghans whose voices
are too rarely heard.[4]

Hazarajat, Central Afghanistan, Spring 1997

Evaluating a community development program in Afghanistan's
central highlands, I walk through remote mountain valleys, asking
groups of people to describe their lives, the good times and the
bad times, what they dream of and what they fear. Over and again,
this is what I hear: 'During times of peace, they take half our grain,
the best of our animals, our rugs and yoghurt, our wood and trees.

They take our sons as labourers and our daughters as maids. They take all we have, give nothing back, and expect us to be grateful. During times of war, the government cannot tax us, landlords cannot collect. If we are unlucky, we may be looted, our crops burnt, our sons killed. But perhaps the fighting won't come our way. We may lose one or two sons as soldiers but, God willing, will feed and clothe our other children. During peace time, the cities grow fat while we grow food and starve. In war time, no-one is fat but we starve last. We long for peace, but not any peace.'

Kabul, Spring 2002

Journalists swarm over the city. Over a thousand International Non-Government Organisations, registered since January, compete to move quickest, spend biggest and act most visibly to most dramatic effect. English displaces local languages at coordination meetings, silencing Afghans fluent in other languages. Rentals increase tenfold within a month. A senior colleague observes, 'We've overlooked a major security risk. Families evicted from rented houses will rise up against the foreigners. Why blame landlords for exorbitant rents? Identify the root cause!' The conversation moves to other disasters caused by the plague of expatriates. The water table is falling fast. Wealthy families invest in deeper wells and, as public wells run dry, the children of the poor walk further and further for water. Hydrologists warn that when Kabul's aquafers are exhausted, the city will run dry.

Faryab, Spring 2006

Evaluating a community development project, I learn that tenant farmers pay 75 percent of their produce to absentee landlords. They work the fields all year to feed their families for three months — if rain falls and if other obligations and misfortunes do not extract their produce first. 'Our land is not irrigated. The snows and rains are less reliable than they were: good seasons are less frequent; droughts and floods are more severe and come more often.' How do you survive? 'The travel agents [people smugglers] save us. We send men. The money they send home sustains us. If Iran and other countries close their doors, we are finished.'

Balkh, Spring 2006

A village elder remembers grapes, pomegranates and almonds, fruits his grandchildren have never tasted. Theirs was a land that flowed with milk and honey once. 'In the time of our grandfathers this country was green: trees, gardens, fruit and vegetables, sheep, cows and goats, chickens and ducks. That was before the road was built, before the city, before the aqueduct. As the city grew it drank more and more water and left us with less and less. Our river ran more slowly, it became a trickle, then it stopped . . . We hear that people in the city grow flowers, that some people have so much water they swim in it . . . When our water dried up, we dried up. We are scorched, burnt-up people.'

Nangahar, Spring 2009

Visiting recently resettled valleys, I ask returnees, 'Why did you leave?' This is what I hear: 'There was peace of a sort under King Daud, but not since then. It's always the same. Those in power hold the cities and the plains, the resistance, mujahedeen or insurgents, hide in the mountains. We're caught in between. We get shot when we go out to plough, tend our sheep or collect water. Women and children are not safe inside or out. And young men? The army conscripts them by day; the mujahedeen or Taliban take them by night. When we moved our families to Pakistan, men returned to plant our fields in Spring and to harvest in Autumn. With no one to care for the land and the irrigation canals, our orchards died. With no one to protect the forests, they were pillaged and plundered.' Women lead me to an orange grove. Fifty ancient citrus trees concealed by crumbling mud walls survived the years of exile fed by an underground stream: sweet oranges, sour oranges, lime and other fruits whose English names I don't know. Treasured stock from which new trees are cultivated. Some replanted trees bore fruit this year. The forests — cedar, oak, juniper and pine — tell a less hopeful story. Their remnants are still being plundered.

The ADF claims that Australia's mission in Afghanistan was 'to support the Afghan Government help contain the threat from international terrorism'.[5] How and why did those who authorised this mission imagine that a military intervention would do anything but exacerbate that threat? How and why did they ignore the inevitable human and ecological consequences of war?

57

Ethicist Margaret Somerville believes that we suffer from selective historical amnesia: failures of human memory, a reluctance to tell stories and over-reliance on reason as *the* 'way of knowing'.[6] She advocates other ways of knowing that engage our bodies, hearts and spirits, as well as our minds. Reason, when used alone is ethically inadequate because it operates within and is constrained by the conceptual and categorical constructs of the dominant culture. As Carol Fontaine puts it, reason is 'captive to socialization, teaching us *not* to see what needs to remain hidden for ideological purposes'.[7]

Might Australia's intervention in Afghanistan be a consequence of 'the widespread failure of empathetic imagination' that Somerville laments? Are we captive to an ideology of war that renders failure invisible, even inconceivable? Might other ways of knowing enable our leaders to acknowledge that escalating cycles of violence will not and cannot bring peace? Will they learn the humility to respect and learn from those whose lands and lives their decisions have blighted?

Imagination is one other way of knowing. Walter Brueggemann defines 'prophetic imagination' as 'the human capacity to picture, portray, receive and practice the world in ways other than it appears to be when examined through a dominant, habitual, unexamined lens'.[8] Jean Paul Lederach understands the 'moral imagination . . . as the capacity to imagine something rooted in the challenges of the real world yet giving birth to that which does not exist'.[9] This capacity 'emerge[s] from and speak[s] to the hard realities of human affairs [yet] finds a way to transcend [and] move beyond what exists while still living in it'. The moral imagination perceives things beyond and at a deeper level than is immediately visible or audible and attends in an embodied way — sensually, spiritually and intuitively — to present and past realities. It senses how everything relates.

The challenge presses in upon us. Will we, collectively and with our leaders, muster the courage to recover the ancient discipline of repentance and turn away from self-seeking destructive ideologies and habits? Will we, collectively and with our leaders, cultivate the moral imagination needed to seek more just and peaceful ways of being in the world?

---

1. Australian Government, Department of Defence, 'Afghanistan — Operation Highroad', https://www1.defence.gov.au/operations/highroad (accessed 10 Jan 2021). In April 2021, Prime Minister Scott Morrison announced that the remaining Australian troops would be withdrawn from Afghanistan, in line with the US decision to withdraw their troops; Georgina Hitch, 'Scott Morrison Announces Withdrawal of Australian Troops from Afghanistan', *ABC News* Online (15 April 2021), https://www.abc.net.au/news/2021-04-15/scott-morrison-announces-withdraw-australian-troops-afghanistan/100071606 (accessed 28 April 2021).
2. Ian McPhedran, 'Under Heavy Security, PM Tony Abbott Visits Afghanistan and Declares War is Over', News Corp Australia network (29 October 2013), https://www.news.com.au/national/under-heavy-security-pm-tony-abbott-visits-afghanistan-and-declares-war-over/news-story/70f050dca2c5 3cf2e03df04572a030ed (accessed 10 Jan 2021).

3. Statistics here and following from UNData, 'Afghanistan Country Profile' and UNESCO Institute for Statistics. Available at http://data.un.org/en/iso/af.html and http://uis.unesco.org/country/AF (accessed 10 Jan 2021).

4. Conversationalists gave me permission to share their stories to help other people learn more about their lives and their country. For security reasons, the names of people and specific locations are not used. Translations of Dari conversations are my own. I depended on translation into Dari when other languages were used. Although all translations paraphrase, I have retained original idioms where I could. The first conversation fragment is a collation of common themes and patterns of speech from two weeks of discussion with dozens of community groups. The last conversation fragment is from a single group discussion that was typical of my other discussions in those valleys at the time.

5. Australian Government, Department of Defence, 'Afghanistan — Operation Highroad'.

6. Margaret Somerville, *The Ethical Imagination: Journeys of the Human Spirit* (Melbourne: Melbourne University Press, 2007).

7. Carole Fontaine, 'Watching out for the Watchmen (Song of Songs 5.7): How I Hold Myself Accountable', in *The Meanings We Choose: Hermeneutical Ethics, Indeterminacy and the Conflict of Interpretations*, ed. Charles Cosgrove (London: Continuum, 2004), 105, emphasis in original.

8. Walter Brueggemann, *Hopeful Imagination: Prophetic Voices in Exile* (Philadelphia: Fortress, 1986), 2–3.

9. Here and following, John Paul Lederach, *The Moral Imagination: The Art and Soul of Building Peace* (Oxford: Oxford University Press), ix–x, 26–29.

_____

Further Reading and Viewing

— Australians for War Powers Reform (AWPR). 'A Call for War Powers Reform in Australia'. Be Sure on War, https://www.besureonwar.org.au/about-us/ (accessed 1 February 2021).

— Lederach, John Paul. *The Moral Imagination: The Art and Soul of Building Peace*. Oxford: Oxford University Press, 2005

— Somerville, Margaret. *The Ethical Imagination: Journeys of the Human Spirit*. Melbourne: Melbourne University Press, 2007

— Stewart, Rory. 'Afghanistan: The Great Game — A Personal View by Rory Stewart: Parts 1 and 2.' BBC May 2012, https://youtu.be/6a7bP49ehKQ and https://youtu.be/j6jItZF5ZeU (accessed 1 February 2021).

— Storie, Deborah. 'War Will Not Bring Peace.' *Sydney Morning Herald* (29 December 2008), https://www.smh.com.au/politics/federal/war-will-not-bring-peace-20081229-76db.html (accessed 1 February 2021).

_____

Alex Skovron Hands

What hands are these? To whom do they belong?
Why do they droop as if resigned, or trapped?
What is that yellow pleated cord, can it be strong

Enough to bind them both, could it be snapped
If the two hands would clench and pull apart?
But wait! The right hand's fingers — oddly gapped,

As though half-trembling, twisted, scarred
From some ordeal? And the thumb — is it lost,
Or subtly concealed by the camera's art?

And then see how wearily the hands lie crossed,
Each along each, to nourish the blackness
Glaring behind their pallor, hands of a ghost,

Or sheer despondency, a defeated slackness
That sickens the will, pushing hope aside?
And have these hands arrived from some luckless

Encounter, or about to be taken on a silent ride
To nowhere? To travel forever — or only as long
As our heart is wanting, and our hands are tied?

—————

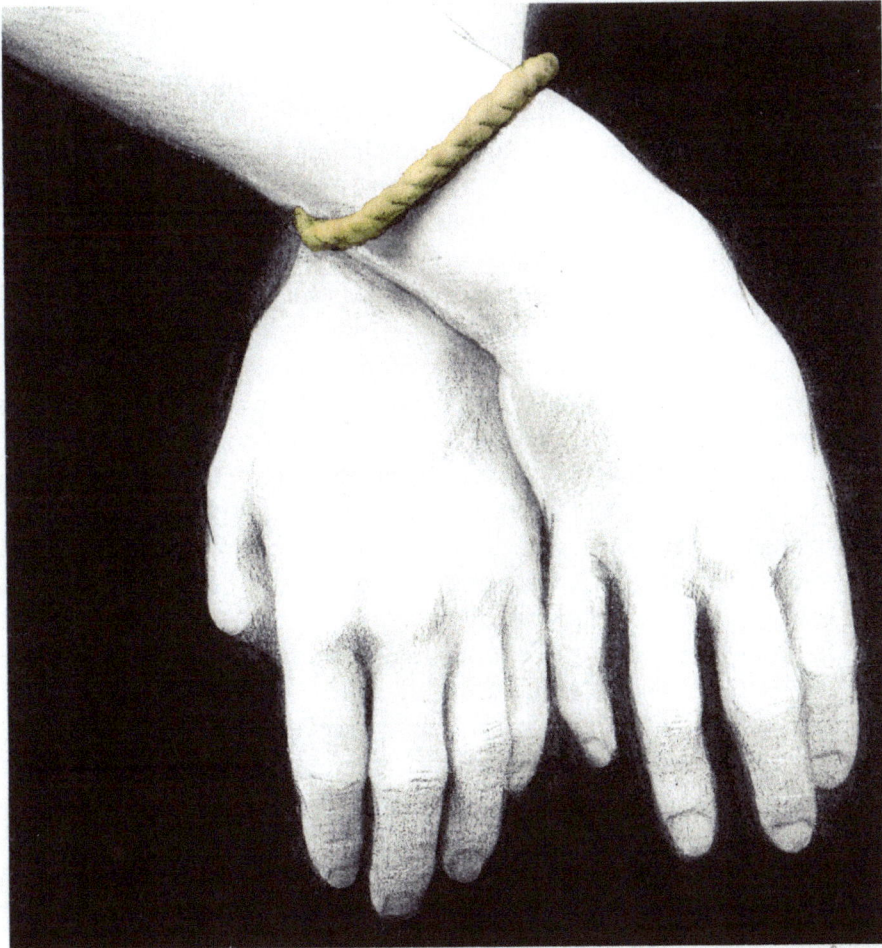

2/3   the Arrival   kelly

William Kelly **The Arrival**

2014, hybrid print: linocut, digital relief print on archival paper, 12 x 18 cm.

The pair of tied human hands in William Kelly's *The Arrival* is intriguing. At an obvious level it suggests oppression, the loss of power and freedom. The poet Alex Skovron notes this in his accompanying poem in which he describes the hands as drooping 'as if resigned or trapped'. For Australians at the present time the artwork, and its title, might initially evoke the trapped situation of refugees, or of detained Indigenous people. Yet when attention moves from the hands to the cord other responses also become possible.

It might be expected that a cord binding hands would be portrayed as some kind of shackle or fetter that is heavy, strong or rough — but the cord here is more finely threaded, a slender and perhaps flexible bond, a gentle cord. As Skovron says, its strength is uncertain. A gentle cord might be the type we would choose for ourselves if we were seeking to willingly bind our own hands. But why would anyone choose to bind their own hands, to willingly restrict the things they might do? Before the 2020 pandemic this might have been a more compelling question but is one that has now been interrogated somewhat as a consequence of the restrictions on individual freedom — on the whole consented to by Australians — that have been necessary to control the virus. The value of limiting freedom is especially significant at the present time when the limits of Earth's natural systems have been so stretched, and often exceeded, that humankind now faces the strong likelihood of social and ecological collapse, or catastrophe, even extinction.[1] Self-limitation might be an important option for those individuals, communities, and nations seeking to reduce the human ecological impact.

Yet difficult thoughts and feelings can be evoked by the idea of intentionally limiting human behaviour. It may seem inimical or perverse to voluntarily restrict our options, because the assumptions and desires that characterised the Enlightenment era — freedom, certainty, progress, growth, optimism — continue to be attractive, familiar and powerful. In the West, their manifestations are everywhere — advanced technology, industrialisation, individualism, the consequences of colonisation, 'growthism'. These manifestations of Enlightenment values are ambiguous. They have led for many to a loss of autonomy, to poverty and diminishment while at the same time for others they have led to substantial benefits in the form of freedom of choice, prosperity, leisure and comfort.

Even in a (mostly) wealthy country such as Australia the idea of voluntary self-limitation can be hard to accept because it appears to cut across the hard-won (though still only partial) victories of oppressed groups and classes (labour, women, people of colour) and contradicts the deeply held modern value of human freedom. But it lies at the heart of the present ecological context. It is precisely the freedom of some to change the face of the earth that has given rise to the present crisis. The freedom of individuals and corporations has sanctioned a plethora of ecological excess and abuse which now threaten to undermine the systems which support life on Earth.

Restraint of all kinds, including self-restraint, does by definition involve some limitation of freedom, but in the present ecological and existential crisis it is hard to see other options. If people choose to take up the cord of restraint as they have done with the pandemic, to gently tie their hands, then it might lead to practical and ecologically beneficial outcomes.

Using a social justice principle, the cord might first be employed by those of us who already enjoy comfort and choice and who also bear the brunt of responsibility for climate change. A globally flat scale of self-limitation would unfairly impact groups and societies which have contributed the least to escalating global emissions but which are the most likely to experience climate change's first and worst impacts.

Individually, privileged Westerners might, as an example, choose to bind their own hands (gently but firmly) by limiting (or ceasing) travel by air. It may seem that 'everyone' flies, but only 20% of people in the world have ever flown, and in the UK, for example, 15% of the population accounts for 70% of flights.[2] Individual action of this kind can empower the individual and contribute to carbon reduction at an aggregate level. At a larger-scale communal or national level, with Australia as one of the world's largest exporters of coal, governments and some corporations are currently poised to vastly increase global emissions. In June 2019 Federal and Queensland governments approved the controversial Adani (now called Bravus) mine in the Galilee Basin which will export 10 million tonnes of coal annually: digging of the main pit began in September 2020 and the construction of 200 kms of railway began in December 2020. Other coal mines are proposed in the Galilee Basin and along with the Bravus mine, production of up to 295 million tonnes of coal a year is predicted, more than doubling Australia's coal exports.[3]

The strong commitment to large volume fossil fuel mining on the part of Australian politicians and many voters is an example of an ideology and practice to which restraint might be applied. This would entail the Australian government taking responsibility for the country's future indirect carbon emissions, prohibiting new coal and liquified gas projects, closing present ones, and re-thinking Australian identity not as a powerful mining country but as a producer of renewable energy. In a similar way Australian identity might be re-thought in relation to its treatment of refugees and Indigenous people.

The Arrival is open to various interpretations which do not necessarily exclude one another — after all, the histories, geographies and politics of refugees and of Indigenous Australians often have deep and extensive ecological roots. The hands in Kelly's drawing might be my hands, the hands of my local community, the hands of wider society, or of the world. Could a soft and gentle cord be something we could willingly learn to use to bind our hands in certain times and places in order to restrain forms of behaviour which dispossess others and exceed the limits of Earth?

---

1. Collapse, catastrophe and extinction are three possible future scenarios discussed by Jem Bendell, 'Deep Adaptation: A Map for Navigating Climate Tragedy', *IFLAS Occasional Paper*, no. 2 (2018): 19–21.

2. George Monbiot, 'History Will Be Kind to Heathrow Climate Protesters Who Stop Us Flying', *The Guardian* (4 September 2019), https://www.theguardian.com/commentisfree/2019/sep/04/history-kind-heathrow-climate-protesters-stop-us-flying (accessed 13 January 2021).

3. Mark Ludlow, 'Courageous or Cut-throat: Adani Changes Name to Bravus', *Financial Review* (5 November 2020), https://www.afr.com/companies/mining/courageous-or-cut-throat-adani-changes-name-to-bravus-20201104-p56bfz (accessed 4 March 2021); Jemima Burt, 'Adani Could Be "Ice-breaker" for Six More Proposed Galilee Basin Mines, Resources Body Says', *ABC News* Online (12 June 2019), https://www.abc.net.au/news/2019-06-12/adani-approval-could-be-galilee-basin-ice-breaker/11194510 (accessed 13 January 2021).

———————

Further Reading

— Bendell, Jem. 'Deep Adaptation: A Map for Navigating Climate Tragedy'. *IFLAS Occasional Paper*, no. 2 (2018): 19–21.

— Burt, Jemima. 'Adani Could Be "Ice-breaker" for Six More Proposed Galilee Basin Mines, Resources Body Says'. *ABC News* Online (12 June 2019), https://www.abc.net.au/news/2019-06-12/adani-approval-could-be-galilee-basin-ice-breaker/11194510 (accessed 13 January 2021).

— Krien, Anna. 'The Long Goodbye: Coal, Coral and Australia's Climate Deadlock'. *The Quarterly Essay* 66 (2017), https://www.quarterlyessay.com.au/essay/2017/06/the-long-goodbye/extract (accessed 13 January 2021).

— Monbiot, George. 'History Will Be Kind to Heathrow Climate Protesters Who Stop Us Flying'. *The Guardian* (4 September 2019), https://www.theguardian.com/commentisfree/2019/sep/04/history-kind-heathrow-climate-protesters-stop-us-flying (accessed 13 January 2021).

— Simpson, Lindsay. *Adani: Following Its Dirty Footsteps: A Personal Story*. North Geelong: Spinifex, 2018.

— Wright, Ronald. *A Short History of Progress*. Toronto: Anansi, 2004.

———————

Peace is more than merely the opposite of war. We wage war, and build engines of destruction, but we make peace, an ongoing, organic process of reciprocity and flourishing. A cease-fire is an end to violence but not hostilities. A victory that comes with reparations leads to ongoing injustices, like the war reparations required of Germany after WWI which aided the rise of fascism. Now the military-industrial complex is big business. A 2020 article by the Stockholm International Peace Research Institute notes that in 2019, the sale of arms by the top 100 arms producing and military service companies reached $1917 billion.[1] The website army-technology.com notes that in 2018, global arms sales were worth nearly US$400 billion.

Imperial and neo-imperial nations wage war on enemies we invent to extract their natural resources, which in turn fuels (quite literally) the machinery that makes war on the planet. To abandon war as a strategy of growth means abandoning violence against the other, particularly the Indigenous other, and the other-than-human. We need to abandon our unjust claims on the resources of others, our carbon colonialism. Australia is not without guilt here, as ally of the US in the wars in Iraq and Afghanistan, in dealing underhandedly with Timor Leste in a bid to steal its oil and gas, or extinguishing the native title (a shadow of proper land rights) of the Wangan and Jagalingou people to enable Adani to mine coal on their land.

Recognising the unjust nature of our claims means identifying our idols and our privilege, and being willing to sacrifice them in the name of peace. Making peace is costly. The flip side is the recognition of the dignity and rights of the other.

Biblical Christianity has resources for this transformation. While the Bible contains texts justifying military conflict, and the history of the church is littered with violence, the figure of Jesus reminds us of the foundational nature of peace to the Christian faith. Jesus declared the peacemaker blessed and called for non-violent resistance to military power. Turning the other cheek to a foe was a provocative demand to be struck as an equal, not with a demeaning backhander. The cross, which features on Christian churches, is not just a reminder of Jesus' death for human sin, but a model for a sacrificial, peacemaking life.

Possibly using an early hymn, St Paul wrote of Jesus' abandoning of his privilege, a self-emptying, or to use the Greek, *kenosis*:

> though he was in the form of God, [he] did not regard equality with God as something to be exploited, but emptied himself, taking the form of a slave, being born in human likeness. And being found in human form, he humbled himself and became obedient to the point of death — even death on a cross. (Philippians 2:6–8 NRSV)

Jesus became a slave and, like a rebellious slave under the Roman empire, was crucified, a thoroughly humiliating and shameful death. He became a human, setting aside his status as equal with the God of Israel in order to both make peace between humans and God, but to be the example of what it is to be a peace-making human. We learn further from the fourth gospel that Jesus took on flesh, an identification with all creatures, not just humans.

Theologians such as former physicist John Polkinghorne further argue that kenosis goes to the heart of the nature of God. The very act of creation is an act of making room for the non-divine other. God seeks relationship with the other that is free to love or not, to turn outward in kenosis towards God and the other, or inward towards the self. Such is the model we need for our relationship with the other. To be kenotic is to love sacrificially, to recognise our privilege and set it aside for the sake of the other, human and more than human. Economist Kate Raworth holds these two in tension in her 'doughnut economics' which recognises the just demands for human flourishing for all, but a respect for the Earth system and the diverse creatures from which it is made.

Kenosis in this sense, however, was not a Roman value. The first century CE community at Philippi to which Paul wrote was a Roman colony, made up of army veterans. As a Roman colony with Roman culture, it was a world where humility was not a virtue, but looked down upon. Instead, the display of wealth through a system of benefaction set up a series of relationships of dependency. The higher up the social ladder you were, the more you were to spend in building a network of dependency, and the louder you had to be about it. Trump would have fitted in well. Furthermore, as a Roman colony, it would also have operated off the back of slave labour. Hence, Paul's audience consisted of those who needed to empty themselves as slaves, and those who already understood what it was to be a slave. To understand Paul's varied audience enables us to both accept the criticism that kenotic thought has been applied shotgun-like, hitting the already disempowered, and shows us a way forward in its laser-like application to the powerful.

Climate change impacts are felt the most by those who have contributed the least, the global poor. The 'age of discovery' marks the beginning of the ideological roots of the Anthropocene and human domination of the planet. Capitalism was spawned in an era when nature, and those regarded as closer to it such as women and non-Europeans, were 'othered' in the name of progress and profit. Today, the impacts of climate change are still gendered and racist. In northern India, melting glaciers and irregular monsoonal rains are causing more damaging floods. Men are forced to leave for the cities to find work, while women left behind are at risk of being bonded into slavery or marriage. The Sioux at Standing Rock are vilified and prosecuted for trying to protect their lands and water from oil pipelines. African Americans were the most affected by Hurricane Katrina, whose flooding impacts were made worse by rising sea levels associated with climate change.[2] Recently, close connections between climate change, the Anthropocene, and COVID-19, have been observed both in terms of causes, and continuing global inequality.[3]

The call to kenosis is therefore not an ethic to be applied equally and at all times to all people, but to the rich, the powerful, the privileged. Paul's hymn continues:

> Therefore, God also highly exalted him and gave him the name that is above every name, so that at the name of Jesus every knee should bend, in heaven and on earth and under the earth, and every tongue should confess that Jesus Christ is Lord, to the glory of God the Father. (Philippians 2:9–11 NRSV)

In this biblical framework of thought and belief, those who are humbled will be exalted, but those who are exalted must first make peace with those they willingly or knowingly humiliate, by emptying themselves. These emptyings mean abandoning some desires: for conquest, success, territory, endless growth, material comfort, many offspring. For those who have been humiliated, this means exalting in recognition as a beloved creature of God, the image of God, their right to flourish, empathy in their struggles, restorative justice in their unjust situations, and a louder voice in the discussion about our shared future. As ecofeminist Priscilla Eppinger states, a kenotic ethic means 'care for marginalized and powerless people who frequently are those most affected by disruption to and destruction of ecosystems'.[4] In the Australian context, this is Aboriginal people, whose connection to Country is profound and, as Christian leader and Waka Waka woman Brooke Prentis often reminds me, who are unaffected by the dualisms that haunt western Christianity. Bruce Pascoe points us to the fact that Aboriginal peoples have managed, and lived with the other-than-human for tens of thousands of years. Their voices need to be heard, we need to exalt their understanding and wisdom, and be willing *kenotically* to set aside some of our own.

---

1. Dr Nan Tian, Alexandra Kuimova, Dr Diego Lopes da Silva, Pieter D. Wezeman and Siemon T. Wezeman, *Trends in World Military Expenditure, 2019*, Stockholm International Peace Research Institute (April 2020), https://sipri.org/publications/2020/sipri-fact-sheets/trends-world-military-expenditure-2019 (accessed 4 March 2021).

2. On slavery and climate change in India, see Mick Pope, *A Climate of Justice* (Reservoir: Morning Star Publishing, 2017), chapter 3. On treatment of the Sioux and arrest over protests see for example Jesse Phelps, 'Two Native Americans Arrested Over Keystone XL Protests', Common Dreams (8 January 2021), https://www.commondreams.org/newswire/2021/01/08/two-native-americans-arrested-over-keystone-xl-protests (accessed 4 March 2021). On sea level rise and Hurricane Katrina see for example Bobby Magill, 'Katrina: Lasting Climate Lessons for a Sinking City', Climate Central (26 August 2015), https://www.climatecentral.org/news/katrina-climate-change-sinking-ground-19370 (accessed 4 March 2021). On social inequality and Katrina, see Naomi Klein, *This Changes Everything* (London: Penguin, 2015).

3. On the scientific and political links between COVID-19 and climate change, see for example Jeffrey Frankel, 'Covid-19 and the Climate Crisis are Part of the Same Battle', *The Guardian* (2 October 2020), https://www.theguardian.com/business/2020/oct/02/covid-19-and-the-climate-crisis-are-part-of-the-same-battle (accessed 4 March 2021). On inequality in vaccine delivery see Patrick Wintour, 'World's Poor Need Action, Not Covid "vaccine nationalism", Say Experts', *The Guardian* (23 January

2021), https://www.theguardian.com/world/2021/jan/22/worlds-poor-need-action-not-covid-vaccine-nationalism-say-experts (accessed 4 March 2021).

4. Priscilla E. Eppinger, 'Christian Ecofeminism as Kenotic Ecology: Transforming Relationships away from Environmental Stewardship', *Journal for the Study of Religion* 24, no. 2 (2011): 47–63 (56).

——————

Further Reading

— Eppinger, Priscilla E. 'Christian Ecofeminism as Kenotic Ecology: Transforming Relationships away from Environmental Stewardship', *Journal for the Study of Religion* 24, no. 2 (2011): 47–63.

— Pascoe, Bruce. *Dark Emu*. Broome: Magabala Books, 2018.

— Polkinghorne, John. *The Work of Love: Creation as Kenosis*. Grand Rapids: Eerdmans, 2001.

— Pope, Mick. 'The Self-emptying Godhead: Perichoresis, Kenosis and an Ethic for the Anthropocene'. In *Ecotheology and Nonhuman Ethics in Society: A Community of Compassion*, edited by Melissa J. Brotton, 81–98. Lanham: Lexington Books, 2016.

— Raworth, Kate. *Doughnut Economics: Seven Ways to Think Like a 21st Century Economist*. London: Cornerstone, 2018.

——————

In the winter of 2019, while we were deep in drought, the hills began to burn.

A dry lightning strike started the fire in the state forest, up in the hills behind our property. Years of drought had dehydrated the soil, the trees and the waterways. Now, most of the creeks were bone-dry; smooth stones marked a path of desire where once the cool water bubbled and bounced its way. Deep in the gully, some birds still sang or called at least, and the kangaroos came close. Our soil was grey dust, rising at every kiss from the wind, smearing the boundary between land and sky. I would think of the spores and bacteria that give the soil life and wonder about their reincarnation, or if they were leaving forever.

The fire smouldered away, all winter and into spring. A little map on my phone showed the boundaries, the changing geometry in two dimensions of a fire that was cleaning out the foreigners — the lantana especially — leaving greasy black smoke to smear the sky but grace the sunsets with colour. Down the crevasses it crept, fingers of fire-front that would stop at the creek, we thought. Each afternoon I'd look up to the hills, brow crinkled, waiting for it to be done. The fire trucks couldn't get access to it, so I hoped the creatures at least could get out, away from the flames. It was winter, it was slow. I hoped the fire was cool and the forest would be safe.

For decades we've known that climate change is a threat multiplier. It makes what once might have been isolated incidents like drought or bushfires more likely, and when they do come, worse. Longer, hotter summers and less rainfall mean there is no longer a safe window for small, cool-fire burning off for hazard reduction in the tradition of First Nations ancestors. Less commitment to public services like state forest management, weed control, threatened species protection, fire-trails and rural fire services, despite the *increasing* need, means that these factors become linked together, piling on each other, creating perfect storms. It's what makes climate change a 'wicked problem': if there is a solution at all, it requires many different types of strategies at different levels all pulling together.

Morally wicked too, I think. This is the work of our own hands, the choices humans have made. The tools we have made to help us exert power over each other, capitalism, colonialism, corporations, are turned against the very Earth, our home. And now she burns. The Australian fires of 2019–20 blazed for 9 months, creating firestorms and megafires never before witnessed. Unbelievable images of whole villages huddled at the ocean's edge, prepared to escape into the water should the fire chase them there. Massive pyrocumulonimbus clouds formed above the intense heat, crazy with lightning and sucking the flames ever upward into an inverted hell. And the dark. The greasy orange grey of days turned red then black like Pharaoh's plagued sun and the apocalypse at once. Dietrich Bonhoeffer used the phrase, 'the ambiguous twilight of creation', and it never seemed so real as those days of dark sky. The mixing of the two lights, the *Zwielicht*, the inseparability of blessing and curse, *tob* and *ra,* when our paradise homes are burning with hellfire.

On New Year's Eve 2019, a blanket of smoke rolled into Canberra and smothered the city, leaving it with the world's worst air quality for many days. The smoke would circle the Earth, smudging glaciers and snowfields before returning to smother us again. By the time the rains came in late January and February to cool the soil and douse the flames, a new darkness was on its way. New viruses that cross species were another consequence that the climate scientists had warned would be more likely.

Gasping for breath became the theme of 2020: first the fires, then the pandemic, another Black man with a knee on his neck, and in a wicked reprise, the West Coast fires of the US. These sins are linked. Our attempted mastery through technology and colonialism and estrangement from our Mother Earth: all of these are connected to our original sin of wanting to dominate the other.

While we held our breath and stayed in our homes, we wondered if humanity would take this last chance to stop polluting the sky with carbon. For a moment, we took stock of the impact of humans on Earth and we listened to the voices of schoolchildren and we thought this just might be the sign, the wake-up call, to decarbonise the economy. We stopped flying, and driving to work and, for a while, the air was clearer and the nights were hushed. And in this quiet, while parliaments were in recess and elders on ventilators, more coal mines were approved.

What would it mean for those of us who are Christian to bring the gospel to all of creation? For humans to bring *good news* to the forests and the air? To let the oceans flourish and for the creatures to live their best lives? To recognise that the God who came to us in the Garden and on the cross remains with us through creation? The God who presses us to bring reconciliation to the world! What would it mean to speak words of love and restoration and through our actions show hospitality — a sharing of our selves with our fellows? Christians might pray for God's 'kingdom to come' (in the language of the prayer of Jesus), for Earth to be as Heaven to us, and yet not recognise that the Earth is burning and suffocating at our hands. We might better pray for the 'kin-dom': a kinship that reflects both our relationship within, and our particular responsibilities on behalf of, the biosphere. We are more like *Homo cosmicos* than the 'wise ones'.

The horror of the future bears down on the present. Predictions are made real, prophecies fulfilled. Climate change is being visited upon us here and now, not to a poor country with sea levels rising and refugees fleeing on boats, but to all of us. People of faith have within our traditions the resources to name climate change as a manifestation of sin. We have the experience to know that 'domination' of Earth and Earth's creatures dressed up as biblical 'dominion' is hubris and a perversion of the Garden story. And yet we have theologies of relationality, of deep ecology, to reframe our relationships in the world. The

Christian God of Trinity, of relationships of love and generosity, is the image in which creation is formed.

Christian hope of resurrection comes to us and restores our souls when we breathe fresh air again and watch the forests regenerate. Our deep, deep sadness over the loss of 3 billion creatures in the Burning Summer can only be countered by the hope that comes from communities defying the odds and pushing back against the trajectory. When we pray for God's kin-dom to come, we enlist to be part of a movement that won't let our home burn and our fellow creatures become extinct, or allow islands to submerge.

Further Reading

— Anderson, Pat, Sally Gardner, Paul James and Paul Komesaroff, eds. *Continent Aflame: Responses to an Australian Catastrophe*. Armadale, Vic.: Palaver Press, 2020.

— Deverell, Garry Worete. *Gondwana Theology: A Trawlooloway Man Reflects on Christian Faith*. Reservoir, Vic.: Morning Star, 2018.

— George, Dr Tommy, et al. *Fire and the Story of Burning Country*. Text by Cape York Elders and Community Leaders Photographed and Recorded by Peter McConchie. Cyclops Press, 2013.

— Kaylock, Julia, and Denise O'Hagan, eds. *Messages from the Embers: Poetry Anthology from the Australian Bushfires 2019–2020*. Black Quill Press, 2020.

— Steffensen, Victor. *Fire Country: How Indigenous Fire Management Could Help Save Australia*. Richmond, Vic.: Hardie Grant Travel, 2020.

Anna Sakurai Cloud Climbers

'It's much too dry out here.'

Without a single foot outside,
The steely motor humming,
Kangaroos that came for grass
Lie headless by the road.

On soil bleached sandy by the sun,
Parched lips trace words to hoarse horizon.
Will we hear the songs of wisdom
That helps us find our way?

Stinging, bloodshot, weary eyes,
Through singed and furrowed brow,
See fear and faces whitened,
Brick clinkers, windows empty.

Star maps flicker up above
Forgotten daily threads,
Hard stakes driven deep within
Fence dreamings from the 'burbs.

Soft feet on settling embers,
Step carefully onto the land.
As smoke lifts a darkened cloud,
Who sees what can be seen?

———————

———————

When I arrived in Melbourne, I felt the ease of being amongst friends. A comfort and lightness. Something that I hadn't realised that I missed. And yet, it seemed so important to risk a different conversation. With those who hadn't noticed yet, how parched the land had become. Such deadly conditions had spread, often with our own consent.

I write this as a frequent traveller, one who makes the calculation. That some trips are worth the miles burnt. But how long can we continue?

As I was honoured to make closing remarks on a most memorable colloquy, I remember asking out aloud, whether we needed night to fall, for us to see the stars, to navigate towards the light, in enlightenment. Now months have passed, in fear for many. I wonder whether we will choose to forget, or to tread more mindfully.

There are many who light the way, especially amongst First Nations elders. We who have come to this land later must now do more than listen. We must stand and walk in solidarity. For any other way, we know, will prove catastrophic.

Compassion, truth and wisdom are not an option. They are a necessity.

———————

Further Reading
— Kwaymullina, Ambelin. *Living on Stolen Land*. Broome: Magabala Books, 2020.
— Reid, Duncan. *Time We Started Listening: Theological Questions Put to Us by Recent Indigenous Writing*. Adelaide: ATF Theology, 2020.
— Yunkaporta, Tyson. *Sand Talk: How Indigenous Thinking Can Save the World*. Melbourne: Text Publishing, 2019.

———————

William Kelly **Peace Not War / Bridge Builders**

c. 2018, digital print on archival paper, 37.5 x 28.5 cm.

Millions gathered in capital cities and rural centres around the world on Friday 20 September 2019 as part of a general strike invited by School Strike 4 Climate.[1] In my home city of Melbourne, around 100,000 people attended, and more than 300,000 nationwide.[2] The numbers in Melbourne were the strongest since the Gulf War protests in 1991. News on climate change as an anthropogenic phenomenon has been around for decades. Its list of effects on human and other-than-human communities arrives under headings of rising seas, displaced peoples, increases in extreme weather events, wildfires, drought, habitat and biodiversity loss, and major levels of species extinction. As the 2017 Roundtable: 'Climate Change Is a Feminist Issue' attests, ecological trauma, social injustice and the lives of women are for feminist theologians a central part of the complex entanglements of human and other-than-human lives and habitats under climate change.[3]

In Australia, there is an ongoing pull toward coal mining, especially mega coal mines gaining state and federal government support in far north Queensland; this is of a piece with the reality that elections in Australia can be won on the basis of racist border protection policies and practices, fear-mongering around rural job losses, and the ongoing logic and practices of extractivism on Indigenous lands. All this was evident in the May 2019 federal election. In late 2019, in a long struggle by the Wangan and Jagalingou Family Council leading the Stop Adani campaign, native title was denied and Indigenous leaders bankrupted due to legal fees, in order to smooth the way for Adani to mine coal in Queensland's Galilee Basin. A coda to this is the way corporations and governments promote a divisive politics in and between Indigenous communities, in order to claim support from traditional owners by being selective about which parties they have discussions and make agreements with.

Contemporary environmental degradation, especially the state of Australian river systems, is being called out as a new wave of genocide. Moreover, as Melbourne-based Indigenous scholar Tony Birch argues, racist stereotyping of Indigenous people, colonial dispossession and climate change are linked, through the violent legitimation of mining on Country. Disastrous effects of climate change are not new for Indigenous people, but part of the ongoing experience of invasion as a system rather than a past event. 'We've Seen the End of the World and We Don't Accept It', says Murrawah Johnson an Indigenous spokesperson for the Wangan and Jagalingou Family Council. The late environmental humanities scholar Deborah Bird Rose describes this ongoing invasive colonial ideology as a dual war against Earth and Indigenous people, 'that includes both genocide and ecocide'. Anne Pattel-Gray, whose work on racism, including in the churches, has not received the attention it deserves in Australia, spoke in Sydney in July 2019 on the need for restorative justice and treaty in the context of addressing the ongoing conflict between invaders and Indigenous peoples; this has implications for ecological regeneration.[4]

In concert with intersectional analyses by scholars of colour, such as bell hooks, Elisabeth Schüssler Fiorenza's critical description of kyriarchy is a useful analytic tool which can be applied to thinking on the complex intersections of patriarchy, racism, classism and ecological trauma.[5] The concept has been taken up by Behrouz Boochani, a Kurdish journalist from Iran to describe 'The Kyriarchal System' that keeps asylum seekers and refugees imprisoned.[6] This system is inseparable from the racism and colonialism that intersect with ecological destruction in Australia. A kyriarchal system of interlocking relations — of sexism, racism, class and the toxic operations of consumer, corporate capitalism — is a descriptor for intersectional analyses of complex relations of power producing anthropogenic climate change, its denial, and current political inertia in Australia with respect to adequate and effective response.

To feminist liberationist analyses of entangled power relations should be added an understanding that other-than-human agencies are also at work in the release of carbon into the atmosphere; while climate change is human-induced it occurs as a result of networks of human and other-than-human actors and properties.

Liberationist analyses foreground experience, education and activism in partnership with First Nations and other local peoples — I am thinking of the work of Ivone Gebara, Hilda Koster and Joyce Ann Mercer.[7] Recognising First Nations sovereignties in colonial contexts, engaging with Indigenous experience and knowledges in ways that are Indigenous-led, is, as both Ellen van Neerven and Birch point out, essential to climate change action.

Critical feminist liberation hermeneutics invite and include creative responses and resistances and should open to creative work arising from women, especially First Nations women, in response to climate change. For example, the poetry of Marshall Islander Kathy Jetnil Kijiner who read 'Dear Matafele Peinem' at the United Nations Climate Summit Opening Ceremony in 2014; and work by Indigenous writers from Australia, such as Natalie Harkin.

There is a need, also, to listen to Indigenous critiques of popular activist movements such as Extinction Rebellion. In 2019, some Extinction Rebellion activists espoused a desire to be arrested in service of the cause; this is being seen as deeply problematic and tone-deaf to the ongoing realities of colonisation in an Australian context where Indigenous deaths in custody continue despite its being nearly thirty years since the Royal Commission into Aboriginal Deaths in Custody handed down its findings and recommendations. Finally, there is a phenomenon in Australia, but not only here, of violent speech, especially through social media, targeting Indigenous women activists against racism, women in the churches writing to support LGBTI+ groups, and climate activists such as Greta Thurnberg. While the impact of climate change, and the politics of anthropogenic climate change denialism, remains a feminist issue, in Australia there can be no climate justice without a shift toward foregrounding the epistemologies, experience and sovereignty of Indigenous peoples.

1. 'Biggest Climate Mobilisation in Australia's History as 350,000 Students + Workers #ClimateStrike', News, SS4C (20 September 2019), https://www.schoolstrike4climate.com/post/biggest-climate-mobilisation-in-australia-s-history-as-300-000-students-workers-climatestrike (accessed 29 October 2019).

2. 'Global Climate Strike Sees "hundreds of thousands" of Australians Rally across the Country', *ABC News* Online (21 September 2019), https://www.abc.net.au/news/2019-09-20/school-strike-for-climate-draws-thousands-to-australian-rallies/11531612 (accessed 29 October 2019).

3. Laurie Zoloth, Elizabeth Allison, Melanie L. Harris, Michal Raucher, Theresa A Yugar, Juan A Tavárez, Alan A Barrera, Alyssa A Henning, 'Roundtable: Climate Change Is a Feminist Issue', *Journal of Feminist Studies in Religion* 33, no. 2 (Fall 2017): 139–75.

4. The Drought, *Q&A*, ABC (28 September 2019), https://www.abc.net.au/qanda/podcast/2019-28-10-podcast/11647706 (accessed 29 October 2019); Bruce Shillingsworth, a Muruwari and Budjiti man, speaks at the 46.00min spot on the podcast. Kyle Powys Whyte, 'Is It Colonial Déjà vu? Indigenous Peoples and Climate Injustice', in *Humanities for the Environment: Integrating Knowledge, Forging New Constellations of Practice*, ed. Joni Adamson and Michael Davis (London: Routledge, 2017), 88–105; Wangan and Jagalingou Family Council, https://wanganjagalingou.com.au/ (accessed 9 July 2019); Deborah Bird Rose, *Reports from a Wild Country: Ethics for Decolonisation* (Sydney: UNSW Press, 2004), 34; Anne Pattel-Gray, 'Restorative Justice', Common Dreams 2019, https://2019.commondreams.org.au/public-address/restorative-justice (accessed 29 October 2019).

5. I note that women scholars of colour to whom Elisabeth Schüssler Fiorenza refers in relation to the development of her critique of hierarchical dualism/kyriarchy include Barbara Smith (ed.), *Home Girls: A Black Feminist Anthology* (New York: Kitchen Table: Women of Color Press, 1983); bell hooks, *Feminist Theory: From Margin to Center* (Boston: South End Press, 1984); Cheryl Johnson-Odim, 'Common Themes, Different Contexts: Third World Women and Feminism', in *Third World Women and the Politics of Feminism*, ed. Chandra Talpade Mohanty, Ann Russo and Lourdes Torres (Bloomington: Indiana University Press, 1991), 314–27. See Elisabeth Schüssler Fiorenza, *But She Said: Feminist Practices of Biblical Interpretation* (Boston: Beacon Press, 1992), 8–9, 220, nn. 17 & 18.

6. Behrouz Boochani, *No Friend But the Mountains: Writing from Manus Prison*, trans. Omid Tofighian (Sydney: Picador, 2018). In his introductory, 'Translator's Tale: A Window to the Mountains', Omid Tofighian writes, 'the notion of kyriarchy amplifies the extent and omnipresence of the torture and control in the prison' (xxvii).

7. Ivone Gebara, *Longing for Running Water: Ecofeminism and Liberation*, trans. David Molineaux (Minneapolis: Augsburg Fortress, 1999); Ivone Gebara, 'A Reform That Includes Eco-Justice', trans. Marcos Brias, *Dialog: A Journal of Theology* 55, no 2 (Summer 2016): 117–21; Ivone Gebara, 'Women's Suffering, Climate Injustice, God, and Pope Francis's Theology', in *Planetary Solidarity: Global Women's Voices on Christian Doctrine and Climate Justice*, ed. Grace Ji-Sun Kim and Hilda P Koster (Minneapolis: Augsburg Fortress. 2017), 67–79; Hilda P Koster, 'Trafficked Lands: Sexual Violence, Oil, and Structural Evil in the Dakotas', in Kim and Koster, eds, *Planetary Solidarity*, 155–75; Joyce Ann Mercer, 'Environmental Activism in the Philippines: A Practical Theological Perspective', in Kim and Koster, eds, *Planetary Solidarity*, 287–307.

Further Reading and Viewing
— Birch, Tony. '"We've Seen the End of the World and We Don't Accept It": Protection of Indigenous Country and Climate Justice'. In *Places of Privilege: Interdisciplinary Perspectives on Identities, Change and Resistance*, edited by Nicole Oke, Christopher Sonn and Alison Baker, 139–52. Leiden: Brill, 2018.
— Boochani, Behrouz. *No Friend But the Mountains: Writing from Manus Prison*. Translated by Omid Tofighan. Sydney: Picador, 2018.
— Guess, Deborah. 'Oil Beyond War and Peace: Rethinking the Meaning of Matter'. In *Ecological Aspects of War: Religious and Theological Perspective*, edited by Anne Elvey, Deborah Guess and Keith Dyer. *A Forum for Theology in the World* 3, no. 2 (2016): 73–93.
— Harkin, Natalie. *Dirty Words*. Carlton South: Cordite Books, 2015.

—IPCC: The Intergovernmental Panel on Climate Change, https://www.ipcc.ch/ (accessed 4 March 2021).

— Jetnil Kijiner, Kathy. 'Dear Matafele Peinam'. YouTube, https://youtu.be/DJuRjy9k7GA (accessed 29 October 2019).

— Neerven, Ellen van. 'The Country Is Like a Body', *Right Now: Human Rights in Australia* (26 October 2015), http://rightnow.org.au/essay/the-country-is-like-a-body/ (accessed 27 June 2019).

— The Uluru Statement from the Heart, https://ulurustatement.org/the-statement (accessed 14 January 2021).

———————

Among the many side-effects of colonialism and neocolonialism are environmental degradation and a population struggling to maintain itself in sustainable ways. In Latin America, colonialism meant the conquest and control of other people's lands and goods — experienced brutally though the bodies of women who were raped, African peoples who were enslaved, and Indigenous populations who were wiped out. It also left the legacy of a colonial mentality. What begins as an imposition eventually becomes an appropriation and enactment of a mentality that condones and justifies exploitation, discrimination and enslavement. This colonial mentality leads people to seek individual and immediate gains at the expense of long-term wellbeing and sustainable ways of life.

From the colonial practices of pillaging land and people, enslavement, forceful conversions to Christianity, and robbing human beings of their dignity to modern practices of neocolonialism that benefit international capital (leaving behind a trail of destruction of fauna and flora), Latin American history is a history of institutionalised looting. Exploitative trade deals and political alliances reveal not only a dependence from developing nations on international capital but also the creation of national elites who collaborate with — and benefit from — the exploitation of their fellow citizens by incentivising slash and burn, deforestation, and heavy use of pesticides and herbicides in agriculture. The appropriation of public assets for private gain and the use of personal influence for public prestige are a trademark of our politics and economics. Not democracy, but rather cleptocracy has been the longest running system in the continent.

To a great extent, religion served as ideological scaffolding to justify the sacrifices required from those treated as the least and the last, and as support for the Christendom model of the *Christus Victor*, the victorious Christ associated with European expansion and, more recently, capitalist imperialism. Its most recent iteration is prosperity theology, an ideology that equates health and wealth with divine blessing at the expense of the suffering of others. While the entire creation groans in pain, humanity can no longer obsess with mainstream views of development and theological discourses that condone it. Rather, instead of despair, people are invited to envision sustainable ways of dwelling on the land, embracing ways of life that honour the intersection between economic, environmental and social wellbeing. To enable this, it is paramount to reclaim theological discourses and practices that ensure life in abundance and affirm the dignity of all human beings and the wellbeing of the planet. This can be done by using an ecological approach — studying the *oikos*, the house and the multiple households we inhabit: our personal bodies, social bodies and the body of the entire creation.

The environmental crisis requires theological response, calling churches and communities of faith to denounce environmental abuses and stand by those who are most deeply affected. While contextual, liberationist, black, womanist, feminist and ecofeminist theologies have forged a path in life-affirming initiatives, there is more to be done and learned from environmentally-conscious and Indigenous approaches. One of them is the concept of *sumak kawsay* or *buen vivir* (good living) that is rooted in the worldview of the Quechua peoples of the Andes. This way of life is community-centric, ecologically-balanced and culturally-sensitive because it sees social, cultural, environmental and economic issues working together and in balance. Instead of focusing solely on immediate financial rewards, it considers the wellbeing of future generations in relation to all sentient beings and non-sentient entities.

Current development models have placed a strain on the environment and its inhabitants. Environmental degradation affects plants, animals, soil, water and people. For instance, take the case of illegal mining in the Brazilian Amazon — known as *garimpo*. One can easily see its impact in a broader sense: it involves deforestation, pollution of rivers with dumping of mercury, trade in drugs and arms, alcohol, prostitution and human trafficking. It has negative impact on forest communities as well as the natural habitat. A map of illegal mining in the Amazon, recently released, shows the scale of pollution and damage to the environment, but it also offers a window into the world of crime that mining creates.

Colonialism and neocolonialism do more than extract tribute, goods and wealth from a conquered country; they restructure economies, drawing individuals and communities into a tangled web involving the flow of human and natural resources. They impact the most vulnerable, such as Indigenous populations, who are often treated as an impediment to progress. Nowadays, international capital bypasses 'countries' (which are seen as burdens because of taxation and environmental regulations) by creating supra-national conglomerates that continue the patterns of exploitation. The end result is that, in the name of a free market, profit is extracted and not reinvested locally, while the social and environmental responsibility for clean-ups and treatment of diseases, among other problems, falls on local populations. The outcome is that the most vulnerable are left to fend for their own survival. This environmental injustice is also a theological problem, as certain communities (particularly poor, Indigenous, and people of colour) are disproportionally exposed to pollution and its effects on health and environment with unequal protection and access to the laws, regulations and governmental programs to ensure their wellbeing.

Sustainability — that the needs of the present can be met without compromising the ability of future generations to meet their own needs — is an invitation for action and reflection. It requires that empathy and compassion be extended not only to our current generation (whom we see) but also to future generations (whom we do not yet see). This echoes St John's own words (1 John 4:20–21), proclaiming love towards all of God's children, whether they be near or far. In a time in which immediate rewards trump future benefits and ostentation of material goods surpasses the wellbeing of the *oikos*, there is need for a profound reflection on humanity's purpose and reason to be.

79

Our fixation with immediacy affects how we think sustainably about the resources needed by future generations (and how they are impacted by deforestation, water management, use of pesticides in our foods, etc.) as well as our relationship to other human beings. It demands that we also address the *us* in sustainability, i.e., the human component of it and how it relates to decoloniality. In light of the immensity of problems and urgency in solving them, many people feel overwhelmed and paralysed because there is so much to be done. But while it is true that nobody can address everything that jeopardises the life of the planet, it is equally true that everybody can do something to promote life and its flourishing. Sometimes, it is more manageable to focus on a particular facet of a current issue and from there reflect on its causes and effects on a broader scale. This interlinking and overlapping approach can help us value human dignity and safeguard the wellbeing of the planet.

An alternative to the construction of social and economic 'others' — including nature, the environment, and ecosystems as 'others' — is an intersectional approach in which differences are not used to discriminate, but rather to build coalitions of mutual empowerment and advocacy. Can our theological endeavours create greater awareness about other people's plights, their struggles and hopes? Can they overcome the divide between humans and more than humans? Can they foster common initiatives and activities that promote the type of life together that is at the core of *buen vivir,* where the wellbeing of creatures and creation alike are ensured? Can we imagine and work towards a time and place in which human ability can transform us and the world into a household of hospitality and care for the entire creation? I hope so and trust that, together, we can envisage and strive for this to become reality.

Further Reading

— Balch, Oliver. 'Buen vivir: The Social Philosophy Inspiring Movements in South America'. *The Guardian* (4 February 2013), https://www.theguardian.com/sustainable-business/blog/buen-vivir-philosophy-south-america-eduardo-gudynas (accessed 4 March 2021).

— Collyns, Dan. 'Inside La Pampa: The Illegal Mining City Peru Is Trying to Wipe out'. *The Guardian* (25 March 2019), https://www.theguardian.com/cities/2019/mar/25/la-pampa-the-illegal-mining-city-peru-wants-wiped-out?utm_term=RWRpdG9yaWFsX0d1YXJkaWFuVG9kYXllUy0xOTAzM-jU%3D&utm_source=esp&utm_medium=Email&utm_campaign=GuardianTodayUS&CMP=GTUS_email (accessed 4 March 2021).

— Deifelt, Wanda. 'Out of Brokenness, a New Creation: Theology of the Cross and the Tree of Life'. In *Eco-Reformation: Grace and Hope for a Planet in Peril*, edited by Lisa E. Dahill and James B. Martin-Schramm, 55–70. Eugene: Cascade Books, 2016.

— Galeano, Eduardo. *The Open Veins of Latin America: Five Centuries of the Pillage of a Continent*. New York: Monthly Review Press, 1997.

— Mignolo, Walter. *The Darker Side of Western Modernity: Global Futures, Decolonial Options*. Durham: Duke University Press, 2011.

— Quijano, Anibal. 'Coloniality and Modernity/Rationality'. *Cultural Studies* 21, nos 2–3 (2007): 168–78.

— Santos, Milton. *Toward an Other Globalization: From the Single Thought to Universal Conscience*. Cham, Switzerland: Springer International Publishing, 2017.

Based in Quito, Ecuador, I work across the region supporting local peace-building with a team from Guatemala, El Salvador, Honduras and Colombia. 2020 has been especially challenging of course with the COVID-19 pandemic and the accompanying pandemics of widespread hunger, violence against women, militarisation of civil society and most recently, the very destructive Hurricanes Eta and Iota, powered by climate change, which have affected more than 9 million people.[2] The health, economic and so-called natural disasters have had disproportionately devastating impacts on Indigenous and Afro-descendent communities in Latin America, increasing already glaring social disparities.

So, what have feminist liberation theologies to offer in such a context *in extremis*? I will focus on two themes: salvation and imagination.

Salvation

Ivone Gebara writes of 'successive salvations', moments of happiness, freedom, of 'everyday resurrections' marked by gestures of tenderness.[3] Such gestures of tenderness today are turning into spontaneous heroic acts of courageous solidarity. People are literally saving each other. The myth of an external saviour is gone. No more waiting for outside help from governments, clearly revealed as riddled with corruption. The slogan has returned with force: *Only the people, save the people*.

I share two stories from feminist liberation theologians in the region.[4] From Chiapas, Mexico, Geraldina Céspedes reports that during Hurricane Eta, she left her house to bring food to neighbours, walking through her street which had become a river, with water up to her thighs. Suddenly, she saw a terrible scene: a 9-year-old Indigenous girl, Esperanza, struggling, drowning. Geraldina immediately threw herself into the water, cell phone and all, to save Esperanza, and then carried her home to her mother who was waiting with 5 other small children in a flooded house. Geraldina emphasises: technology died (her cell phone) to save human life.

A second recent story comes from feminist activist theologian, Nelly Delcid, of northern Honduras, whose own house filled with water during Hurricane Eta. She alerted her social networks that she was trapped at home with her elderly mother and a young woman, before her cell phone died. After six hours, the water rose above the windows and doors, the lights went out, and they prepared for the worst. Suddenly, a neighbourhood boy, learning they were trapped, climbed over a makeshift structure to reach their roof where he tore open a hole to rescue them. Nelly cites experiencing her house as a dark watery womb from which she was pulled out through a narrow space into a world filled with daylight, flowing with a current of love. The young boy gently massaged her water-logged legs so she could walk again. She was so struck by his extreme kindness and care.

These are moments of exquisite attention to the fragility of life and death, to the reality of impermanence and radical interconnection. Celebration of life saved and lamentation of that lost, have been key to feminist theological activity in the region, with spiritual gatherings of tens to hundreds of friends and family members for wakes, funerals and other transnational ecumenical and interfaith liturgies online.

Nelly lost almost everything in her house, left in ruins. It was flooded again by Hurricane Iota this week. She is now living temporarily with her sisters, and has immediately begun helping others made homeless, both in her neighbourhood and beyond. Through national women's rights' networks, she is reaching out to rural Tolupan Indigenous women cut off and without food.

Extravagant generosity spirals on, the social fabric continually woven and held in place by everyday resurrections, successive salvations, together seemingly invisibly transforming broader social patterns.

Imagination

Feminist liberation theologies call forth the imaginative impulse, more urgent than ever now. When the strict COVID curfews and quarantines began in March, I met with my colleagues from Central America and Colombia to talk about next steps. We concluded there was nothing we could do, since almost no one could go out. Then, we began to ask ourselves, what if we *could* do something. What would it be? This envisioning allowed us to act. Although under tight legal restrictions, we were allowed out to buy and deliver food. So, we began to prepare peace baskets, with food, medicine, messages of hope and emergency phone numbers, especially to women at high risk of violence. Later we added seeds to the baskets, and then home vegetable gardens began. Envisioning unleashes the energy of life — and that creativity is contagious.

This creativity has been especially true with Kichwa women colleagues in the Andean Highlands;[5] they immediately moved from food delivery, to home gardens, to collective gardens of high-protein beans, chochos, and exchange of agricultural products and seeds. An economy based on sharing and collaboration, not greed and competition.

Imagining that another society is possible, is deeply rooted in memory, in ancestral wisdom. In the Andes the Indigenous cosmological vision is strong: Sumak Kawsay, living well in harmony, reciprocity and balance, respecting the multiple dimensions of time/space: humans, deities, ancestors and nature.

Yet during the pandemics, most Latin American countries have been under an extended State of Exception, with many basic constitutional rights waived, including the right to assemble and protest in large groups. This has facilitated governments' ability to take controversial steps, such as, illegally conceding additional ancestral territories to extractive industries without community consent.

In the face of the huge challenges, a clear call has emerged from Indigenous feminist theologians, like Bolivian Aymara leader, Sofia Chipana, who remind us of the long legacy of foremothers who preserved and maintained life, leading us to honour the wisdom of ancestral spiritualities as resources to recreate a world of justice.[6]

With Sofía Chipana, Patricia Gualinga of Ecuador and Lorena Cabnal of Guatemala,[7] we remember that the feminist struggle for justice is the struggle to defend and preserve land territories, body territories, and that ecological violence is a form of violence against women.

We proclaim feminist justice as cognitive justice, decolonising epistemologies to embrace corazonar, thinking with the heart, and senti-pensar, feeling-thinking.[8] Corazonar, senti-pensar, in everything we do, from teaching to ministry to activism. In this way of knowing and being and acting together, we can save ourselves and our planet.

1. This essay is based on remarks given at the Feminist Liberation Theologians Network American Academy of Religion/Society of Biblical Literature, Online Gathering, 20 November 2020.

2. UNICEF estimates that 9.4 million people were affected by the Hurricanes, with at least 3.4 million in need of urgent assistance. UNICEF, 'Response to Hurricanes Eta and Iota', https://www.unicef.org/reports/response-hurricanes-eta-and-iota (accessed March 25, 2021).

3. Ivone Gebara, *Out of the Depths: Women's Experience of Evil and Salvation* (Minneapolis: Fortress Press, 2002), 121, 124.

4. Special thanks to Nelly Delcid and Geraldina Céspedes for permission to share their stories; email and Whatsapp correspondence with author, 18 November 2020 and 24 March 2021.

5. Members of the women's program, Jambi Mascari (Searching for Health) and its President Magdalena Fueres, of the Union of Indigenous Peasant Organizations of Cotacachi (UNORCAC).

6. Sofia Nicolasa Chipana, 'De la sanación a la liberación', in *Re-encantos y Re-encuentros: caminos y desafíos actuales de las teologías de la liberación*, ed. Dalíns Rufín Pardo and Luis Carlos Marrero (Buenos Aires, Argentina: Juanuno1 Ediciones, 2018), 157–66.

7. Lorena Cabnal. 'Feminista comunitaria, indígena maya-xinka, Guatemala Amismaxaj, Acercamiento a la construcción de la propuesta de pensamiento epistémico de las mujeres indígenas feministas comunitarias de Abya Yala', en *Feminista siempre. Feminismos diversos: el feminismo comunitario* (España: ACSUR-Las Segovias, Asociación para la cooperación con el Sur, 2010), 11–26, https://www.acsur.org/ (accessed 19 April 2021).

8. Patricio Guerrero Arias, *La Chakana del Corazonar: Desde las Espiritualidades y las Sabidurías Insurgentes de Abya Yala* (Quito, Ecuador: Abya Yala/Universidad Politécnica Salesiana, 2018); Boaventura De Sousa Santos, *The End of the Cognitive Empire: The Coming of Age of Epistemologies of the South* (Durham: Duke University Press, 2018).

William Kelly **Dialogue II: Religion**
1987–1993, silkscreen, 61 x 80 cm.

'Dialogue II: Religion' by William Kelly, 1985–93
after a statue of St John the Baptist, Clifton Hill, one mile from Hoddle St

even from here, we knew that sound
wasn't fireworks or a car backfiring
            a kind of tinnitus began in every middle-ear
hairline cracks opened in our skin
                        the air, seismic

                  I was a hundred miles away, but
only three years younger than that man
who hid behind a billboard
            began targeting passing drivers
he opened twenty-six bodies (seven died)
opened another fissure in the earth
            Wurundjeri land

before Hoddle Street happened (the grammar
                  is wrong, there are people, decisions)
he was an army cadet, stabbed his sergeant-major —
            his own face lost blood —
his girlfriend left him, debts mounted up
his blood lost face — so, after
watching a movie at his mother's house
                  he took three rifles
                  and a hundred rounds into us

here, nearby, in remote
communities and across continents — so many human
figures are defaced   their hands are broken
their heads, divorced from bodies
                  who has not felt that cleaving?
                  who has not clung to such a weapon?

and here I am still, face to face
with this figure made of patience and pressure
whose limbs are frozen, whose eyes don't close
            knowing I am one   who turns away
                        to protect myself
                  speechless and ashamed

———

Suggesting that the human voice is a tool for doing good, as well as promoting evil, appears banal. Although this statement is axiomatic, it is suggested here that the response should not be one of resignation, but of asking the question of how we can use the amplification and projection of the human voice for good and to defeat the evil of war? So how we can use the human voice, amplified by the many, and using contemporary communication, international law and the Security Council to promote a reduction of warfare and the use of force. Calling to account those who are now arguably beyond the reach of the law, but perhaps not of public opinion?

While on one hand, weapons of mass destruction (WMDs) in the military sense can create mayhem, death and destruction on a massive scale in winning (or even losing) a war; on the other, the human voice, the word, can teach and change hearts and minds without hurt, maiming, prolonged warfare or the killing of innocents. We need to harness this power to avoid war.

Currently we are led by people who selectively, and often disingenuously, voice facts to devastating personal advantage, including the advancing of their political parties, nation states, the military industrial complex among others, or to promote warfare against unfriendly states, generally with a significantly weaker military machine. Our leaders, seldom or mostly, don't lie outright, reminding us of the aphorism about half-truths. Perhaps it has always been this way, but contemporary communication technologies allow leaders to project their words, and for us to hear them, thousands of miles away, and to do so almost instantly. Perhaps what we as ordinary citizens enjoy, or suffer today, that our ancestors did not, is arguably a helicopter view of many world leaders simultaneously talking about subjects that critically affect our collective wellbeing.

The public's trust in our key institutions, according to the ABC, the Australian Broadcasting Corporation, is at an all-time low. For example, Western leaders used facts selectively in their own parliaments to 'prove' that Iraq was developing WMDs in order to 'legitimise' their invasion of Iraq. They did so against the advice of their own intelligence services and the International Atomic Energy Agency (IAEA) because war suited these leaders politically. Thousands of human lives later, the ongoing destruction in Iraq continues. In practice, the story of the boy who cried wolf, does not resonate. Contemporary leaders are calling for a war against Iran, again on a similar unproven pretext, to prevent Iran from developing nuclear weapons. In practice, it was the USA who withdrew from the legal verification regime that served to prevent any such development in the first place.

Few members of the public believe these leaders, on a nuclear Iran, or anything else for that matter, but we are yet to break free from the orbit of the politicians who simultaneously demonise the refugees and asylum seekers who form a chain of human misery that links back to the invasion of countries like Iraq or Syria.

On a different topic, many Anglophone leaders also deny the effects of global warming, which in the past anyway was largely caused by the rich 'North' (or the 'Western world'), while again simultaneously denying the cries of those fleeing the rising waters or the effects of intensifying desertification of the already precarious lands of the poorest, exacerbated by a warming planet.

Even institutions which have good reputations are making unfathomable decisions leading to the conclusion that these decisions are politically biased. For example, we have the Nobel 'Peace' prize awarded to President Obama, a man who was leading a nation which at the time was simultaneously conducting two wars in Iraq and Afghanistan. The silence from the world media to such hypocrisy was deafening, or perhaps our societies have internalised the '1984' Ministry of Truth so much that we have become numb and immune to the misdeeds of our leaders as long as it only affects the poor in the third world.

Powerful states also engage in targeted assassination of their enemies living on foreign soil. According to Germany, in 2020, the Russians have allegedly killed a person, deemed a terrorist, in Germany. If the allegations against the Russians are proven true, this is indeed a condemnable act, for the taking of a life without a proper and open judicial process and doing so in a sovereign country. Similarly, when the American government kills someone, for example Mr Baghadi or Mr Bin Laden, also in third sovereign States, without due process, there is general applause in the West for this action. The refrain is that 'we are at war' with terrorism and, therefore, states may use 'all necessary means' to kill opponents in third countries and to do so without a fair and open trial. Such extrajudicial killings in countries not at war, war that is declared, must adversely affect international peace and security (IPS). The Security Council (SC), the pre-eminent body charged by the UN to protect IPS, appears impotent in the face of such transgressions by powerful states.

What prevents the Security Council from condemning such questionable actions and seeking answers from the responsible states? The SC's history helps us understand the situation a little better. Unfortunately, when setting up the SC, the 'world' at that time consisted primarily of the Soviets, the USA, along with their satellite states and a few independent countries. The vast majority of the human population of that time were either not represented at the UN or were represented by their colonial masters. Consequently, the SC was formed, and as a recognition of the *realpolitik* of the time gave the most powerful five nations (P5) the power of veto over SC resolutions. Consequently, when necessary to protect their interests, the P5 acted largely to benefit the national interests of the P5 and their allies! This veto serves the powerful quite well, to silence any condemnation of their activities some of which are morally totally reprehensible, yet legally possible. So, who watches this particular watchdog?

Justice Windeyer of the Australian High Court noted that the law is always 'in the rear and limping a bit' when it comes, broadly speaking, to social issues. This reactive nature of law has worked reasonably well to regulate issues between humanity in the past. The question for our times, however, is whether such a slow reactive system can be effective in situations when humans collectively are affecting the planet in uncontrollable and unforeseeable ways that can generate existential international problems such as global warming or nuclear annihilation. So, the question becomes: How can the slow processes of international law be adapted to enforce change that is equally effective and applicable on the wealthy and the powerful as it does with crushing force on the weak and the oppressed, and to do this by empowering the human voice of 'the peoples'?

The real question for the ordinary citizen, the 'silent majority' or as some would have it the 'great unwashed', is *how can international legal mechanisms be used to project the collective human voice of ordinary people*? A mechanism that surpasses national boundaries, to effectively and lawfully harness this driving force to create broad human custom that will create binding enforceable international law from which the rich, the powerful and the polluters cannot and will not be able to derogate? What is suggested below, it is conceded, is going to be difficult to achieve. The powerful do not relinquish their power, unless forced.

Many have sought to change this paradigm of giving a few powerful nations such as the P5 the veto, this 'get out of gaol free' card. However, the difficulties even of cajoling spent European powers such as the British or the French to give up their right of veto is immense. Thus, the reality is that convincing the USA, Russia (who inherited the veto of the Soviet Union), or the Peoples Republic of China (who was initially 'represented' by Taiwan from 1948 to 1971) to unilaterally give up the veto appears insurmountable. The proof that the UN in the contemporary legal regime would not have allowed states to wield the veto power is the case of India which has agreed not to seek the veto in return for a permanent seat on the SC.

We need to have a mechanism where the SC can be asked to act through public demand (say a million signatures) to force debate on particular matters of international peace and security nominated by the people. We are told that war or the use of force must remain a last resort and that the international public should enforce this laudable aim of the UN. Modern technologies give us the power to demand the SC debate issues that are brought to them by 'the people'. This will not completely stop the powerful of our times, but it may make them pause to consider their actions. The voice of the people of the world can and should demand this voce as a right!

Pondering how best to begin an essay aiming to inspire hope, I'm imagining what life would have been like a century ago. Following a brutal war caused by extreme selfishness and the greed of people with phenomenal wealth and power, the world was in the grips of the deadliest pandemic in human history. Really, in so many ways, civil society has come a long way. We've never understood all that makes up our miraculous and magnificent world and our place in it better. And whether cellular or universal, fascinating new horizons challenging human comprehension and imagination are continuously emerging. And yet, in the blink of a cosmic eye, all life on this planet is on the edge of a cliff. Choices were made; some simply ignorant, some mind-shatteringly calculated and murderous.

As if on cue — fuelled by long forewarned extreme heat and dryness — unprecedented fires were ravaging this giant-skyed ancient land months before we saw in 2020. At first, we anxiously counted the fires followed by firestorms. But then too many were emerging and merging to keep track. Images of giant infernos like the one that raged just north of Sydney during the first official week of summer 2019–2020 are burnt into our collective minds-eye.

As days turned to weeks, smoke thick with chemical fire retardant reached South America. And footage of a woman sprinting through walls of flames holding a koala, nursing the innocent, helpless creature that is our nation's icon, also travelled around the world. All told, 34 people died as more than 18.6 million hectares were incinerated into a massive carbon bomb.[1] The fires ravaged an untold number of ancient, sacred Aboriginal sites and burnt more than three billion animals to death, as well as destroying the natural habitats of survivors.[2] While more than 5,900 buildings were destroyed, we still don't know how many species were lost forever.

Meanwhile, as if fires and floods were invading us from the inside, a long-anticipated microscopic zoonic virus had begun its silent stalk, engulfing the lungs of its human hosts and stealthily advancing around the globe. Collectively — and yet in deeply disturbingly unfair ways — communities all over the world have faced an existential reckoning. As it turns out, unpaid and/or underpaid and often undervalued workers have carried out the lion's share of 'essential services' needed for societies to function. And of course, human and planetary health are entirely interconnected and interdependent. It is a fact that all lives depend on the 'essential services' provided by living ecosystems.

On a global scale, extreme weather — fires, droughts, ferocious storms and floods — and oceans of plastic aside, every measurable ecological health indicator is screaming that fundamental interconnected and interdependent systems holding our 'pale blue dot' together are collapsing. As we come to terms with the latest scientific facts and evidence, the relative handful of humans with the psychopathological profiles that drove us to this horrifying reality are madly scrambling for more power. They are doubling down in their efforts to trawl the planet in search of new resources to crudely (cheaply) extract. Naturally, vulnerable communities on the front line of resource conflicts and climate breakdown are more easily exploitable for short-term financial gains which reap more power.

In fact in the 1950s, evidence from Hawaii's Mauna Loa Observatory was clearly showing that rising greenhouse gases were already melting glaciers. It was in the 1960s that Rachel Carson's mass consciousness-elevating *Silent Spring* mobilised the environment movement. In the 1970s many of the clean energy alternatives, as well as understandings of the natural drawdown technologies that could have averted the now advanced climate and associated biodiversity crisis, were already in development.[3] Meanwhile, the MIT Club of Rome's seminal report *Limits to Growth* supercharged the data showing that endless growth on a finite planet was obviously an impossible equation. While polluters have spent subsequent decades doubling down their efforts to maintain power — in all its manifestations — dedicated, collaboratively-organised teams of scientists and inventors have been making incredible discoveries. Not only have our collective capacities to understand life on Earth advanced astonishingly, but we also know how to undo much of the horrendous harm humans have caused.

So, choices are always being made. The global economy is a fabrication based on choices; a direct reflection of the values that people in power choose to prioritise, and the assumptions and excuses they make in order to justify those choices. Where would we be now if leaders had responded to the clear evidence of the problems as well as the solutions? As the OPEC crisis demonstrated in the 1970s, relying on finite resources that can easily be manipulated for profit and power is unwise at best. In the 1980s the ban on ozone-depleting chlorofluorocarbons (CFCs) was quickly succeeding in repairing the world's dangerously degraded stratospheric ozone. And yet the industries massively profiting from practices that were clearly dangerously degrading our critical ecosystems were being given huge public subsidies to expand their activities.

Can you imagine how environmentalists the world over felt when, on the eve of COP15 (2009), funds that were to kick start clean energy alternatives and natural carbon drawdown projects were instead used to bail out a corrupt financial sector whose recklessness and greed had crashed the global economy?

A decade on, just imagine if soils all around the world were now in advanced stages of repair and regeneration such that they were cooler, held more water and nutrients, were more resilient to droughts and exponentially now more effective at drawing down further excess carbon from the atmosphere? Just imagine the jobs, economy and purpose that even a fraction of those public funds could have brought to vulnerable communities.

Instead, too many leaders continue choosing to accept funds from extractive and exploitative industries to maintain 'business as usual' models that reward selfishness and greed. According to the International Monetary Fund (hardly a haven for leftist greenies, and not counting the cost of losing

Climate Guardians Defending Westernport Bay against AGL's Ecocidal Gas Proposal, February 2021.
Photograph courtesy of Julian Meehan.

the capacity of the Earth to support life), the cost to taxpayers of this so-called leadership is around US$4.7 trillion in global subsidies every year.[4]

For a relative moment in time Australia took an unexpected, visionary turn. Thanks to an enlightened philanthropist with an exceptional head for numbers, a trip in our nation's carefully designed status-quo-guarding political system resulted in a Federal Government that put the wellbeing of its people before the profits of its donors. After the 2010 election resulted in a hung parliament, a key to forming government hinged on the acceptance of a Greens proposal to form a non-partisan multi-party climate change committee (MPCCC) to be guided by experts (in science, health, technology and economics) in designing fair and effective policies to address Australia's escalating health and ecological crisis and to end our nation's global climate pariah status.

Despite (or perhaps because of) the Gillard Government's exceptionally democratic process, the then Coalition's leader Tony Abbott refused to participate and highly publicly and aggressively criticised and frustrated the MPCCC's work at every stage. As a result, what emerged from a gruelling process (including death threats to expert advisors as well as at least one committee member) was The Clean Energy Act (2011). Operating from mid-2012 to mid-

2014 — as a complementary suite of bills informed by experts — Australia's Clean Energy laws were arguably the world's most effective climate and environment protection laws at the time. Not only did Australia's emissions come down significantly and quickly but tens of thousands of new more sustainable jobs were created, and local economies benefited from hundreds of millions of dollars in new investment in the clean energy sector.

Unequivocal evidence of the fast and phenomenal success of the Clean Energy bill is arguably the reason why Australia's political discourse is now fever-pitch-reactionary-crazy. Denying the climate emergency in the 21st century is one thing. Denying the mountain of evidence that the solutions to address the climate crisis create more and more sustainable jobs, better health and prosperity for local economies in ways that benefit all, has demanded another ratcheting up of polluter propaganda.

Apparently designed by its political donors, the Coalition government's COVID recovery plan is to use taxpayers' money to prop up costly, experimental, inefficient and ecocidal so-called 'low emission' technologies that will turbocharge the climate and biodiversity emergency. Expressed another way, a so-called free-market government is choosing to use taxpayers' money to fund projects that will further degrade Australia's environment and the global climate because the private sector won't do so on the grounds that they are not 'economical'.

We must ask: would Federal leaders wilfully ignore independent experts (in energy, technology, science, health, engineering, economics) to instead adopt harmful-industry-friendly measures using taxpayers' money if Australia had a fully accountable Federal Independent Commission Against Corruption?

As history has shown time and again, harmonious human societies do not exist if decent, fair-minded people do not actively participate. It's pretty clear from their short-term and self-serving choices that the people currently in key decision-making positions in Australia do not have our nation's best interests at heart. People with hierarchical, exploitative and power-craving tendencies are dangerous. Just a glance back through human history shows what evil humans cursed with dysfunctional and anti-social traits are capable of. Apparently, no amount of personal power will satisfy people suffering from a narcissistic personality disorder, but therapy could at least help.

As a species, we have never been so threatened or been such a threat. This is a fight for life itself, in all its glorious, interconnected and interdependent forms. Yet, we now have the capacity to truly transform all human societies into locally accountable yet globally aware and conscious communities. Given how easy these empowering choices are now, it's a wicked irony that the abuse of information ('fake news') itself has become arguably the most powerful weapon in the heavy arsenal being used against fair and just democratic processes and systems by those whose extreme wealth and/or worldviews are challenged by basic facts, data and evidence.

Effectively addressing current critical and converging societal problems — deepening inequity within and between nations as well as compounding ecological crisis such as climate breakdown and mass extinction to name a few — demands globally cooperative, democratically organised societies based on facts, fairness and justice that are fundamental to the United Nations' universal human rights enshrined more than 70 years ago.[5] Any and all forms of power abuse must be held to account.

Whether in coverage of unprecedented natural disasters or the global pandemic, daily images of countless people taking enormous personal risks to care for others is a reminder of just how incredibly great humans can be. Hold these images in your mind and — armed with facts, data, evidence and a fair-minded approach — please make a choice to help challenge ignorance, selfishness and greed at all levels. As time for effective action to avert unthinkable climate chaos slips away, who will advance human rights and defend the health of the natural world that all lives depend on if not ordinary decent people? As many social movements have shown, civil society can peacefully and effectively hold power abusers to account. We can call out ecocidal and anti-social practices wherever we experience them, in parliaments, at the banks and superfunds, at political party meetings, at offices of the owners of all forms of media, in the streets and in our homes. We have all the tools we need to start healing our communities, as well as local ecosystems, with care and compassion. We deserve and must demand an economy that works for all people and nature. This now is our clarion call.

1. '2019–20 Australian Bushfire Season', Wikipedia, https://en.wikipedia.org/wiki/2019–20_Australian_bushfire_season#cite_note-ninenews20200114-51 (accessed 4 March 2021).
2. Lorena Allam, 'Grave Fears Held for Thousands of Rock Art Sites after Bushfires Lay Bare Irrevocable Damage', *The Guardian* (2 February 2020), https://www.theguardian.com/artanddesign/2020/feb/02/grave-fears-held-for-thousands-of-rock-art-sites-after-bushfires-lay-bare-irrevocable-damage (accessed 4 March 2021).
3. It is wrong to call this a mass extinction because unlike previous events in our Earth's history when species have died on mass, the consequences of ecocidal industry practices have been well understood since mid-last century.
4. David Coady, Ian Parry, Nghia-Piotr Le and Baoping Shang, 'Global Fossil Fuel Subsidies Remain Large: An Update Based on Country-Level Estimates', *IMF Working Papers* (2 May 2019), https://www.imf.org/en/Publications/WP/Issues/2019/05/02/Global-Fossil-Fuel-Subsidies-Remain-Large-An-Update-Based-on-Country-Level-Estimates-46509 (accessed 13 January 2021).
5. 'The Facts That Define Our Grand Divides', Inequality.org, https://inequality.org/facts/ (accessed 4 March 2021).

Further Reading and Viewing
— ClimActs, https://climacts.org.au/ (accessed 10 February 2021).

Youth in strife-torn and climate-impacted regions have shown themselves to be leaders in creating a better world. This is the experience we had in implementing a model of environmental empowerment in Sri Lanka. The model involves two elements. Firstly, it fosters inner change through nature walks, practicing dialogue, meditation, reflective writing, poetry and drawing. Secondly, it transfers that change to the outer world through team workshops, meetings with local officials and religious leaders, engaging the public on waste, plastic pollution and climate change. The model is now ready to be transferred to other countries. Adoption by groups in India and Malaysia was delayed due to COVID-19, but is expected to occur once the pandemic is brought under control.

A chance meeting in 2010 between the co-authors led to the idea for travellers flying to and over Asia to help financially support a program to empower youth leaders in climate-affected communities. Journeys for Climate Justice was formed in 2011, and the Kelani Nadee Yathra (Journey on River Kelani) led by Kanchana and her group Eco-friendly Volunteers (ECO-V) took place later that year. Since 2011, ECO-V has led seven Yathras (Journeys), some short and others extended to 10 or 12 days. Over 350 youth have participated. The chosen participants demonstrate a willingness to contribute and a capacity for leadership.

Support within the country is mobilised from companies, NGOs and government departments. Government approval and support is crucial in a country like Sri Lanka. Agreements are made about the route for the Yathra, and Government provides practical help, for example, with traffic management.

During the Yathras, participants are immersed in actions that encourage and develop their thinking and caring about others, and about the world they live in. They are guided through nature experiences and daily meditation. They take personal responsibility, for example, in washing their own clothes, sharing meals and living in dormitories as a team. They participate in street drama, talk to local residents and use creative arts (drawings, poems) to express their thoughts about themselves and the Yathra. The final event for each Yathra is a meeting where everyone reports on the Yathra from a personal viewpoint, and presents a project that they intend to work on after the Yathra.

Participants undertake many activities, including lectures and group sessions that reinforce information about environment, peace and justice. Talks are organised with local officials, religious leaders and scout leaders. Experiential learning is encouraged as the participants engage the public through street drama or, for example, when they negotiate permission to post 'no plastics' stickers in shop windows and on vehicles.

The Yathras have made a big impact on the young people, especially as leaders. Changes are evident in personal practices and continuing friendships that endure across religious and ethnic divides. After the program, most participants continue contact with ECO-V and seek advice on their ongoing activities. Some are building up their own environmental teams, promoting eco-friendly practices in their workplaces and lobbying for change by business and government.

A participant in the first Yathra in 2011, Newton had been a Tamil combatant in the civil war. He wrote this poem during the Yathra (translated from Tamil):

> This is a journey that has given a meaning to humanity
> This is a journey that blends beauty of Nature
> This is a journey where beautiful places are observed and this is truly a journey where nature becomes life
> This is a journey that brings shame to those ordered to kill
> This is a journey that brings shame to we who killed people
> This is a journey that changed hatred
> This is a noble journey of peace
> And this is a journey that makes us understand the power of God!

Newton's experience

The 2011 Yathra was a turning point of my life. I learnt about life, peace and kindness and I discovered my great love towards Mother Nature. I only knew how to kill. Now Sinhalese are my best friends. Yathra helped me to discover my inner spirituality.

Today my mind is very peaceful, I don't get angry easily. I love my future thanks to Yathra,

All Yathras are best moments for me. One best moment is meditating inside a forest sitting by a waterfall and listening to sound of water. I never forget that moment. I remember every word of ECO-V theme song and still I cry when I listen to it. I know what inner peace and outer peace is now because I enjoy it.

I try my best to pass all what I learnt from Yathras to next generation. Today I am very proud to see all the plants we planted under my leadership after finishing Yathras and I have my own plant nursery now. ECO-V still supports me and I know I am not alone. I am proud that I took the leadership for 7th Yathra. I am helping other youth to run more Yathras. Because they made me who I am today.

Dhanushka's experience

Before Yathra I hated Tamil people. When we met Newton, I didn't want to talk to him first. But then I understood he is same as me. Eventually we learnt how war took place and all were suffering equally. I didn't like Muslims either. But we met great Muslims who are very friendly and love Nature the way we love it. When we meet now, we don't know who is Sinhala, who is Tamil or Muslim. We help each other to conduct tree planting campaigns. So, this is peace for me. Mother Nature bonded us together. Thanks to Yathras I can understand people and animals and trees equally.

We had this friend on our 7th Yathra, and she said, 'this is the place where my parents got killed during war'. We all got shocked. I felt her pain. I knew that pain has no race ... So that's the best lesson I learnt. Today I love my Tamil friends thanks to Yathras.

I am proud to say that due to the leadership skills I learnt, I was able to lead a team of youth to protect trees that government wanted to cut down (along a road in the Udawalawa area). Also, I am getting ready for 8th Yathra and I have a great team today who are very young and enthusiastic.

Chapa's experience

When I joined with Yathra in 2016, I was so thirsty for learning about Nature. Yathra was something deeper than I expected. I was so happy as I got to know about deep connections with Mother Nature. I experienced it and I found the inner peace through it. That really helped me to come out of box and think about other people and I developed compassion for suffering. This way I found outer peace.

The most memorable experience I had during Yathra was 'Tree talking'. I never felt such love towards trees until I started connecting with them. Today I love trees just the way I love my family. I sharpened my communicating skills and today I am proud to say that I am a good leader with effective communication skills. Thanks to Yathra and then to ECO-V where I started my first job, I am training other young people and conduct programmes for school children. I lead my own Yathra last year with Newton.

Wider impacts

The Yathras are having ripple effects in creating a better world linking peace, justice and environment. Media coverage of the Yathras has been outstanding with national coverage via television and newspapers, as well as local radio and newspapers.[1]

Many youth who were trained under Yathras joined the initially successful campaign to stop building the Sampur coal-fired power station.[2] Also, as mentioned above, to stop cutting trees in local areas for development plans.

ECO-V and Kanchana in particular are now recognised in Sri Lanka and internationally. They receive many invitations to participate in environmental initiatives of government, business and international NGOs. This model of youth empowerment around peace, justice and environment can be readily adapted to conditions in other countries. Supporting the Yathras with funds from people who fly makes much sense, let's call it 'climate justice offsets'.

The message is also being spread by Journeys for Climate Justice, which is dealing with applications for funding from other countries including Thailand, Nepal and Indonesia.

---

1. The first Journey in 2011 received coverage as follows: TV (Swarnavahini, Rupavahini and Derana stations); Radio (Ceylon Svadeshi); 6 newspapers (including the English language *Sunday Observer*). Equivalent coverage was received on later Journeys. See Journeys for Climate Justice, https://www.journeysforclimatejustice.org.au/ (accessed 19 April 2021). For example, Malaka Rodrigo, 'This Year's "Yathra" Organised by Eco-Friendly Volunteers (Eco-V) Saw Youth from the North and South Getting a Firsthand View of the Northern Environment', *Sunday Times* (Sri Lanka), https://www.pressreader.com/sri-lanka/sunday-times-sri-lanka/20180708/283970358204442 (accessed 6 April 2021).
2. 'Sri Lanka to Build Power Plant in Trincomalee', from *The Economic Times*, Energyworld.com (16 September 2016), https://energy.economictimes.indiatimes.com/news/power/sri-lanka-to-build-power-plant-in-trincomalee/54361027 (accessed 6 April 2021).

Further Reading and Viewing
— ECO-V. https://www.facebook.com/ecovsrilanka/ (accessed 12 January 2021).
— ECO-V. https://www.eco-v.org/ (accessed 4 March 2021).
— Journeys for Climate Justice: Empowering Climate-affected Communities. https://www.journeysforclimatejustice.org.au/ (accessed 12 January 2021).

William Kelly **Witness / Cloud Climbers II**

2018, hybrid print: lithograph / digital print, hand coloured on archival paper, 29.5 x 21 cm.

'Witness / Cloud Climbers II' by William Kelly

And he dreamed that there was a ladder set up on the earth, the top of it
reaching to heaven; and the angels of G-d were ascending and descending on it.
(Genesis 28:12)

Witness
         Jacob's angels where we sleep   heads pillowed on our
                        ruin

                     This could be any city
                    torched   any two
                             towers straining
   shorter than these steps

                Each
                  ladder
                    is longer
                      than the
                        next

   (A hand grasps   A foot
         grips the News   rung
             over our polis

The man in front of the tank
         is tall as the tank
reaches halfway the elevation of the towers
                         quaking
                           (We know about the planes
                              The first is lost
                         in fire
                              The second sketched
                         in sky

         Amid trees   wind fills
                a sovereign flag
           Through bands of black and red

                           sun
                     breaks
   on a man and a tank

  and on a single rose
            that scrapes the sky

              ... /

Nearby   a person   palm
to hip   stands on a cliff
overlooks the Earth

Malachei hashalom
descend
upon our sleep

One sits on cloud
edge etched in lead

Sky overwhelms the land
with hatching strokes

A white gap
top right   might open to nothing at all
or to a many storied
climb toward

another way
of ground

———————

Note: *Malachei hashalom* is Hebrew for angels
(or messengers) of shalom (or peace and wholeness).

Hallway and Street. Photo © Pauline Brightling, 2020.

these rhythms of walking   foot
paths   topping

and tailing long days of inside   we're traipsing
unmoored   past our neighbours' fences

wooden picket   Brunswick green wire   low brick
across gutter and macadam past

ornamental plums   shading into a red
and yellow swirling at our feet   while

wattle birds and lorikeets flock and squabble in flowering gums
scattering rosy pinkness like confetti   their raucous calling

filling the street   waking late sleepers or
magpies trawling across grassy verges   listening and   warbling   ... /

to each other   gardens tended
dark soil   freshly turned   silver

beet rising in the salvia bed   and the end
of the roses   caught   for the table

while hips darken towards winter
we greet each other with nods

      and a wide berth
apologetic   our conversations reaching out like streamers

while we move apart
festooning the neighbourhood with looping nets

of touch and hold   and uncertainty
a weave we have never made or

noticed before
it cradles us   together we are   suspended above

fear's turbulent currents
our feet   criss-crossing these streets

these rhythms of walking

—————

Let the mountain be your temple,
The forest — your cloister,
The river — your pilgrim path.

Let the animals be your *sangha*,
The birds — your angels,
The insects — your Indra jewels.

Let elephants be your prophets,
Whales — your gurus,
Dolphins — your blessed assemblies.

Let the desert be your doorstep,
Stars, the needles of beauty that open your wound,
Sky, your liberation.

Let mosses be your worlds within worlds,
Ferns, your lacy raiment,
Fungi, your labyrinth.

Let fossils be your relics,
Boulders, your Old Folk,
Grottos, oracular, your holiest of holies.

By the elements, be tested,
By the terrors, chastened,
By the hungers of predators,
Apprised, as flesh, of your place.

Let walking be your ground-state,
Cognition, communion,
Communion of the human
With its very ground.

Let Earth be your soul,
Its inexhaustible life, your inexhaustible life,
Its mystery, your mystery.

Let your work, your *via activa*, be tending it,
Attending to it,
Learning its Law, turning its pages, deciphering
Its scriptures.

... /

Let planting be your prayer,
Knowing what to plant, and where,
Your wisdom.

Let protecting, preserving, restoring,
Be your worthiness,
Observing its results,
Your bliss.

All there is, is this.
This Law.
Follow its course.
Bushes will burn for you,
Manna will fall,
Pillars of cloud will join you, as escort.

Of revelation, beloved, you will never be short.

————

God of Jesus Christ
we come to you because there is no-where else to turn.
There is a famine in our land, a famine with regard to living
  and telling the truth.

We confess that we invaded this land and enslaved its peoples,
the people who have cared for this country and its waterways
  for thousands upon thousands of years.

We confess that we have wilfully ignored the wisdom of the First Peoples,
wisdom about how to live in this country in a way that honours
  and preserves all life,
that we have trampled their knowledge underfoot and treated it
  with contempt.

We confess that we have treated the land itself with contempt,
  and its seas and waterways also.
We have not cared for it as we ought to have done.
Instead, we have exploited and raped it to feed our selfish appetites.

Now the land is sick.
It weeps and cries out in pain.
Its plants and animals, the rich tapestry of its eco-systems,
  are burning up for lack of nourishment and care.
And it is our fault.

Teach us, O God, to amend both our lives
  and the political and economic systems in which they are embedded.
Teach us to treasure the First Nations of this land
  and their wisdom about how to live here with respect and sensitivity.
Teach us to treasure the country and waterways on which we depend,
  its cycles and seasons, its plants and animals, its fragile and beautiful
  ecosystems.
Teach us to call our political leaders to account.
Teach us, O God, to live and tell the truth.

God of Jesus Christ,
We come to you because there is no-where else to turn.
Have mercy on us and free us from our sins.
Amen.

———

Offered to the settler churches by Garry Worete Deverell,
trawloolway man and theologian from lutrawita (Tasmania, Australia).

Benjamin McKeown & William Kelly **Closing the Gap**
2018, hybrid linocut/digital print on archival paper, 29.5 x 42 cm.

1/15   Closing the Gap

www.ingramcontent.com/pod-product-compliance
Lightning Source LLC
Chambersburg PA
CBHW061136030426

42334CB00003B/57